AF251539

Made by Hand

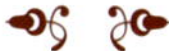

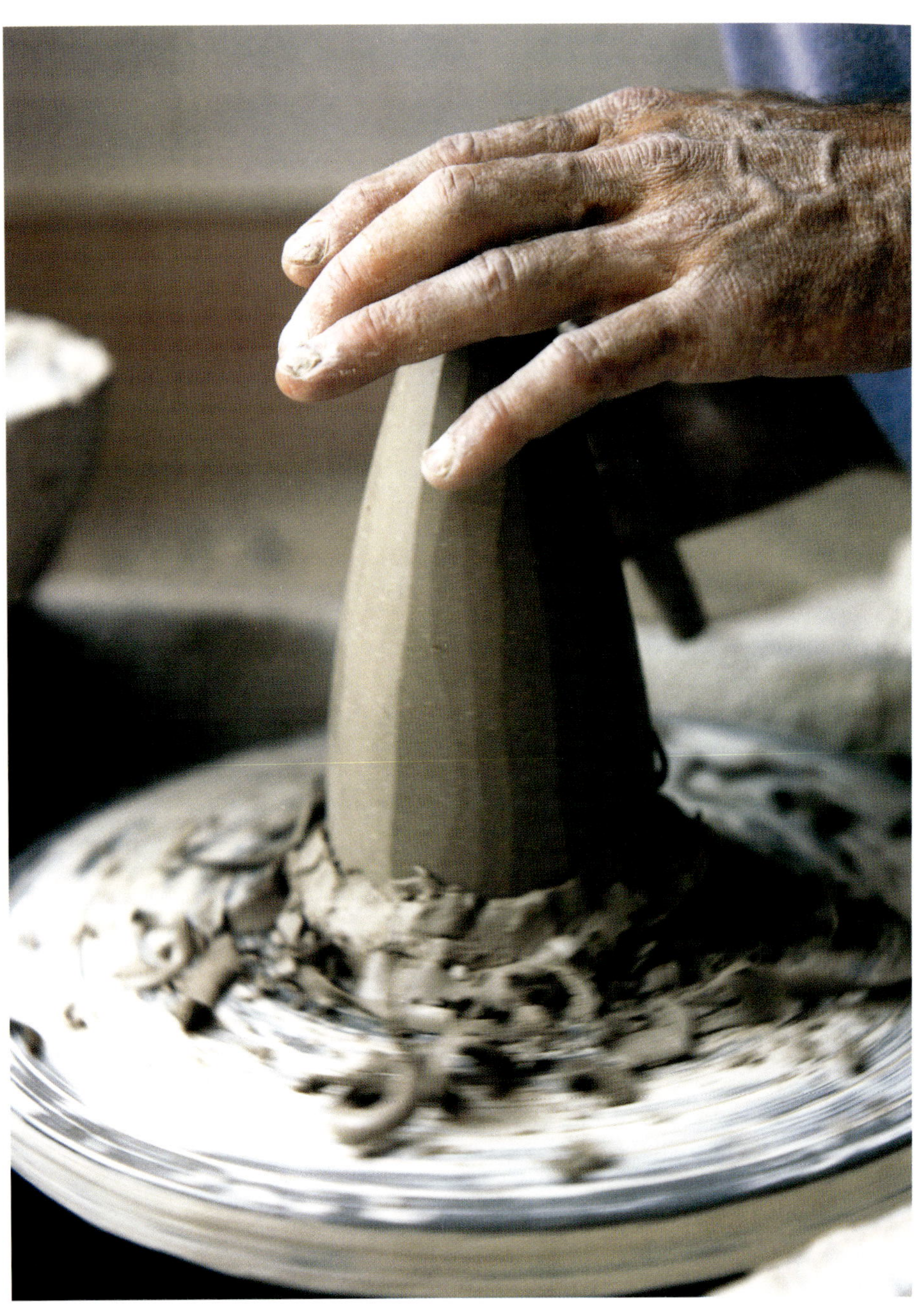

MADE BY HAND

Art and Craft in the Heartland of New England

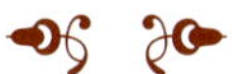

JEANNE BRAHAM

Photographs by Mary Schjeldahl

Commonwealth Editions
Beverly, Massachusetts

ISBN 1-889833-65-7

Library of Congress Cataloging-in-Publication Data

Braham, Jeanne, 1940–
Made by Hand : Art and craft in the heartland of
New England / Jeanne Braham ; photographs by Mary Schjeldahl.
p. cm.
Includes index.
ISBN 1-889833-65-7 (hardcover)
1. Decorative arts—New England—History—20th century. 2.
Artisans—New England—Interviews. I. Schjeldahl, Mary. II. Title.
NK810.B73 2004
745'.0974'09045—dc22
2003020708

Unless credited otherwise, all photos are by Mary Schjeldahl.

The image on the jacket is a detail from "Moses" by Barry Moser from
the Pennyroyal Caxton Bible, used by permission of Mr. Moser.
See page 20 for the entire image.
The quotation by Anne Truitt on page 167 is from
Daybook, The Journal of an Artist
(New York: Pantheon Books, 1982), p. 130.

Design by Dean Bornstein
Printed in China

Published by Commonwealth Editions,
an imprint of Memoirs Unlimited, Inc.,
266 Cabot Street, Beverly, Massachusetts 01915

Visit our Web site: www.commonwealtheditions.com

CONTENTS

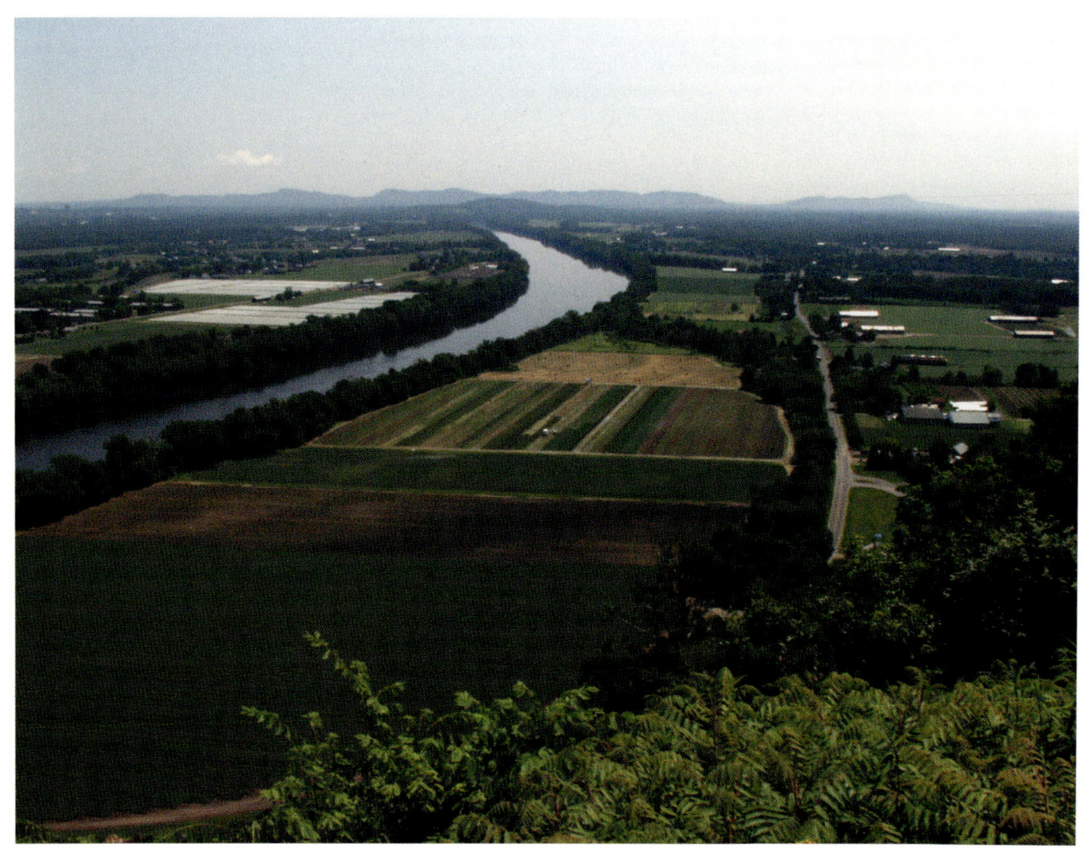

View of the Pioneer Valley from atop Mount Sugarloaf. The Massachusetts section of the Connecticut River Valley, settled in the 1620s and 1630s, was named the Pioneer Valley to reflect its role as America's first inland frontier.

INTRODUCTION

A Sense of Place

THE PIONEER VALLEY: The region is the scene of bloody Indian uprisings, frontier confrontations, spiritual revivals, educational experiments, social communes, artistic flowerings, and some of the richest topsoil in the country. The fertile alluvial deposits forming "Hadley loam" and arranged in one-hundred- to two-hundred-acre tracts are still farmed, in large measure, by the descendants of Polish immigrants who came to the Valley in the mid- to late nineteenth century.

How orderly the villages and patchwork farm fields of the Upper Valley look from one of its mountain precipices: Mount Holyoke, Mount Tom, or Mount Sugarloaf. Yet it is also, in Adrienne Rich's memorable phrase, "the country that broke the heart of Jonathan Edwards, that enclosed the genius of Emily Dickinson," a land full of historical reverberations, contradictions, and diverse ideologies that rub up against one another in companionable and not so companionable friction.

It has been called by many New England's Heartland, a term appropriate not only because of the bounty of its farms, but also because of its equally fertile and nourishing artistic and intellectual communities. In these technologically sophisticated times, communication races across cyberspace with dizzying speed; yet, in the Pioneer Valley, communities are still organized around the river, still bordered by the

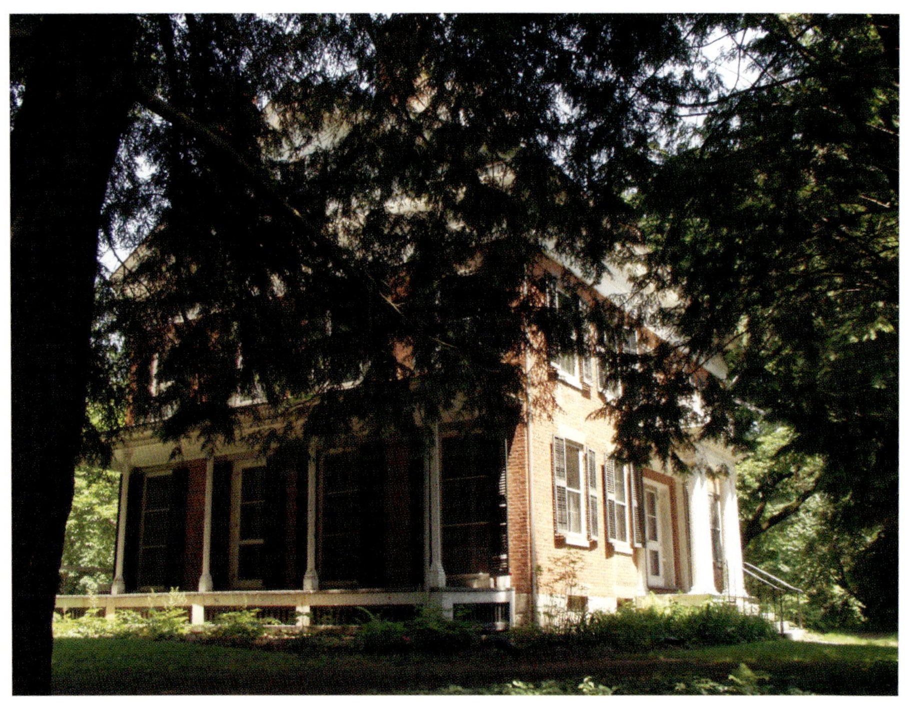

The Dickinson Homestead, probably the first brick house built in Amherst. Now owned by Amherst College and open for tours and readings, the Homestead draws hundreds of visitors each year who want to explore the rooms Emily Dickinson rarely left, the surroundings where she composed her astonishing poems.

thickly wooded hills, still nestled in some traditions as old as the first settlements beyond the eastern seaboard.

Perhaps because the Valley lies in the palm of history's hand, many of its writers focus on its distinct sense of place. Emily Dickinson, New England's premiere literary seer, catches the designs of the universe in the particulars of her backyard garden, slightly to the left and south side of Main Street in Amherst. Richard Wilbur's exquisite and metrically perfect poems often limn the natural landscape around his

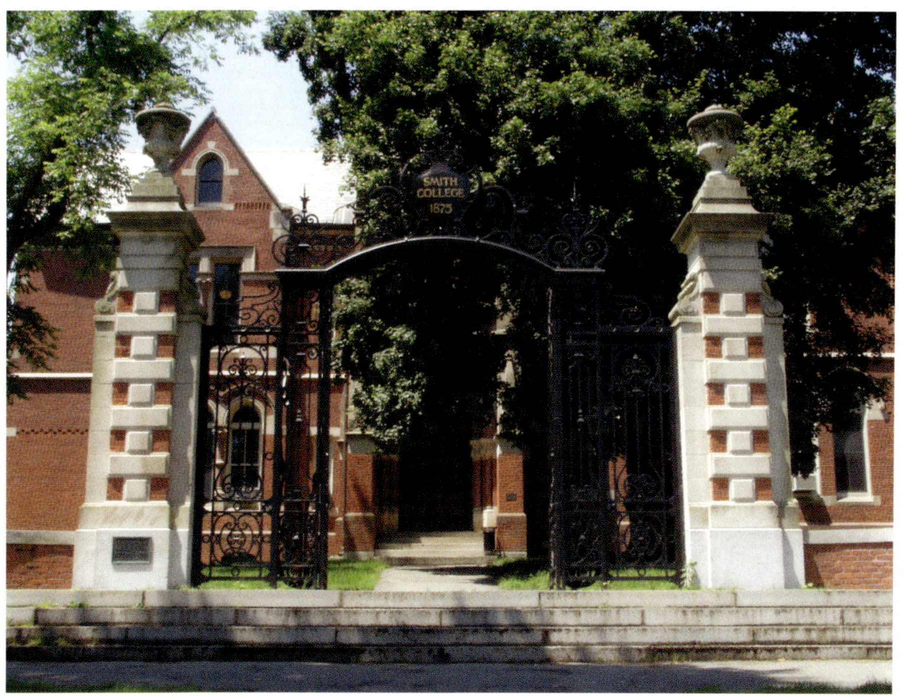

*College Hall and the Grecourt Gates of Smith College dominate the
head of Northampton's Main Street.*

Cummington home and the nearby bubbling Swift River. Tracy
Kidder's award-winning nonfiction tracing the processes of home
building, the credits and debits of nursing homes, and the essential in-
gredients of a hometown are set in and around the small towns of
Northampton and Amherst. In the Pioneer Valley, a sense of place ex-
ceeds simple geography: It stretches backward into history and forward into an evolving state of consciousness.

The industrial communities of Springfield, the largest city in
Western Massachusetts, and Holyoke, a classic nineteenth-century
mill city, dominate the southern portion of the Valley, while intellectual

institutions and academic life are deeply rooted in the north. Noted prep schools like Deerfield Academy, Williston Northampton School, Stoneleigh Burham School, and Northfield Mt. Hermon School are clustered in a fifty-mile radius. Northampton's Clarke School for the Deaf, the first residential school for the profoundly hearing impaired, was founded in 1867, a bold experiment in oral communication. And the Five Colleges, which draw more than 35,000 students to the area, offer one of the most highly concentrated and respected academic communities in the nation. Amherst College, founded in 1819 by Noah Webster and other Congregationalists (who worried about the liberal tenets of Unitarianism sweeping Boston) was soon followed by Mount Holyoke Seminary in 1837 (shortly thereafter renamed Mount Holyoke College) and Smith College (1875), each of which had the mission of providing educational opportunities to women coequal with those available to men at Amherst College. In a massive growth spurt following World War II, Massachusetts Agriculture College exploded into the full-scale educational and research-oriented University of Massachusetts. And Hampshire College, founded in 1970 as an experimental college featuring student-designed majors and "concentrations," based its curriculum on "modes of inquiry," or the process of devising better and better questions. As one of its graduates exclaimed, "If the question mark had not existed, Hampshire would have invented it."

Political and social reform movements were as important as intellectual inquiry in forming the Valley's sense of place. From Jonathan Edwards's Great Awakening and Shays' Rebellion to the abolitionist advocacy of John Brown, Frederick Douglass, and particularly Sojourner Truth—all members of the utopian commune calling itself the Northampton Association of Education and Industry—the Valley crackled with political reformers, arch reactionaries, and plenty of blueprints for fresh visions. A fierce pursuit of the question (however it might be interpreted), regardless of the answer, and a fierce pursuit of

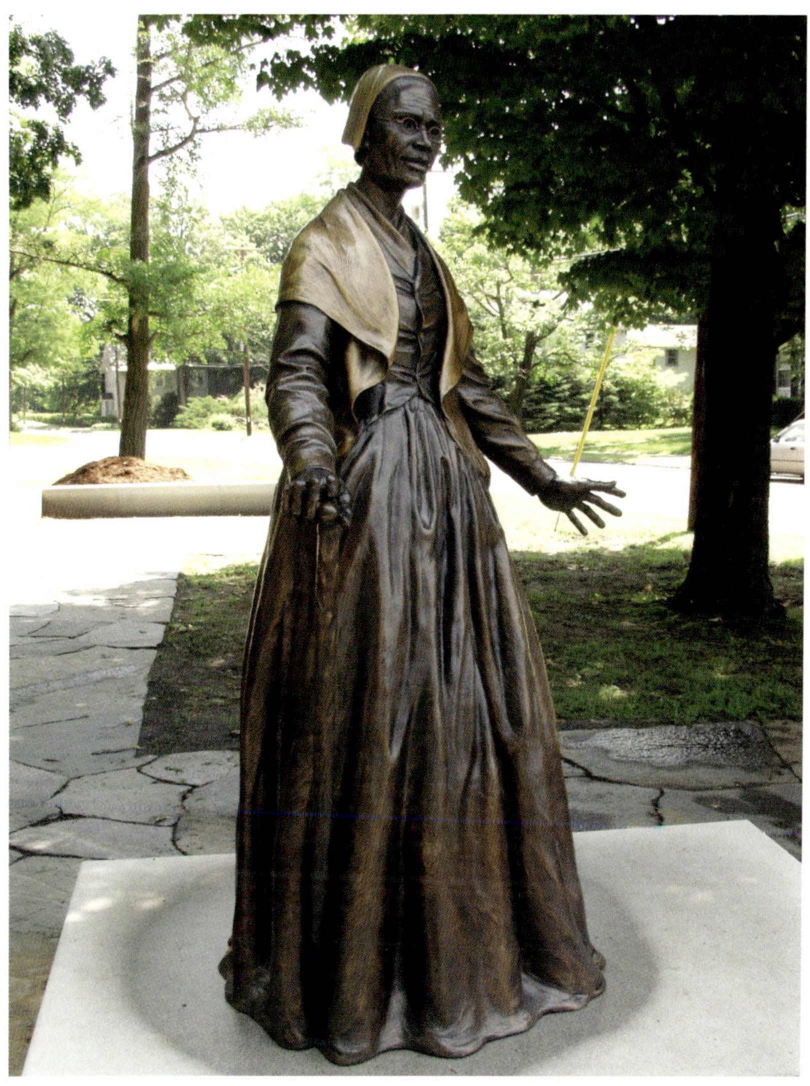

A bronze statue of Sojourner Truth, a former slave who became a nationally known advocate for equality and justice, stands at the corner of Pine and Park Streets in Florence, near the site of the home she occupied from 1843 to1857. Created by sculptor Thomas Jay Warren, the statue was completed in October 2002.

justice (however it might be interpreted), regardless of the consequences, formed the spiritual, intellectual, and cultural backbone of the Valley.

It is not surprising, then, that the Valley has attracted many artists who work in a variety of media and who enjoy the personal freedom the region affords. Personal freedom serves as an important prerequisite to artistic expression, but the practical advantages of the area may have offered even greater enticements. Rents on studio space were—and are—reasonable. In Florence and Easthampton, large industrial mills have been converted into multiple studios and lofts, and many small factories in outlying areas have been rehabbed into studio space. Land remained relatively inexpensive, particularly during the 1970s and 1980s, and many artists were able to buy small farms in the beautiful hill towns surrounding the river valley. And when one factors in the many teaching opportunities available in multiple secondary schools, colleges, and the university, it becomes clear that the Valley offers optimum conditions for the development of a thriving arts community.

Many Americans are familiar with painter Thomas Cole's *The Oxbow* (1836), a painting depicting the view of the Connecticut River Valley as seen from Mount Holyoke, an iconic and idyllic picture of civilization coexisting in gorgeous equipoise with nature. History records many more clashes, disharmonies, and open rebellions than Cole's romantic vision would suggest. Yet, the Valley is, in ways that matter to artists, a place where a vista view is possible, where individual vision can seed itself and, with luck and persistence, can grow.

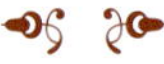

The promise of a flourishing arts community brought me to the Pioneer Valley in the summer of 1989. Leaving behind a tenured professorship at a good liberal arts college in Pennsylvania, I traveled to Amherst, Massachusetts, my fledgling Heatherstone Press in tow, determined to find the rich community of artists, writers, and printers I had read about and longed to join. Smith College had hired me to teach several courses during the fall semester and I would be spending the spring semester at Hampshire College facilitating two seminars in American literature and culture.

I could hardly believe my luck. The figures who inspired my greatest literary passion—Dickinson, Melville, Hawthorne, Thoreau—all lived and wrote in Massachusetts. For years I had used my vacations to travel and to photograph those places where they had produced incandescent work, places I reasoned "spoke" for them: the House of Seven Gables, with its startling proximity to the sea; Arrowhead, where Melville positioned his writing desk so as to see Mount Greylock "rising like a whale"; Old Deerfield, which in my mind's eye ran red with blood; the site of the church in Northampton where Jonathan Edwards preached his riveting sermons until banished to the wilds of Stockbridge, in the Berkshire mountains; the location in Florence where a revolutionary commune held, if briefly, the volatile spirit of Sojourner Truth; and the stately brick Dickinson Homestead where I imagined scraps of writing paper escaping from an upstairs bedroom window. While I was delighted to commune once again with these familiar literary spirits, I also sensed the less visible, but palpable, presence of a thriving artistic community.

Western Pennsylvania was far from an artistic wasteland, but I was wholly unprepared for the depth and range of the artistic community clustered in the Pioneer Valley and its surrounding hill towns. At first, my interest in fine arts presses took me to the doorstep of local printers, illustrators, bookbinders. But as I began to attend local arts festivals—which seem to occur almost every week during the summer and fall months—I uncovered an intricate network of artists and craftspeople, arguably the largest such concentration in the country, producing work of the highest caliber. And as someone interested in storytelling, intrigued by handmade processes, I discovered a story worth telling.

I found myself especially drawn to artists who work in media rooted in New England and who use time-honored methods to create their art: hand tools, wood-fired kilns, handmade engravings, letterpress printing, hand-dyed cloth, quilting, free-blown glass. And while many artists in the Pioneer Valley produce beautiful work, the ten artists who appear in these pages had unique appeal for me: They were superb craftspeople; they had devoted several decades to perfecting their art; they created one-of-a-kind pieces, often calibrated to the needs or desires of their customers. Although they came to the Pioneer Valley for diverse reasons, they stayed and succeeded through some combination of artistic tough-mindedness and vision, perhaps the very qualities embedded in their artistic predecessors, the real pioneers in this heartland of New England who knew the value of what is "made by hand."

Supposing that the artists I chose to interview might be possessed of few words, preferring to speak with their hands, I was delighted to discover that to a person they were articulate, witty, careful with definitions, and full of insights. As one explained to me, "We're people who are shut up for hours and hours alone, inside our shops and studios, often 'out behind the barn.' When we have a chance to talk about what we do and with somebody who really cares, then a river flows."

Some of the interesting currents in that river occur in the conversations that follow. Mary Schjeldahl's photographs offer a parallel narrative as they portray the artists at work, their studios, and some of the work that they create. Finally, art objects themselves "speak" to those who care to listen. They are a crucial part of this story.

BOOK ARTS

PAPER PRODUCTION emerged as a major industry in the Pioneer Valley in the 1800s, and some historians suggest that the presence of large and commercially successful paper mills in Springfield, Holyoke, and Dalton encouraged and supported the growth of private and commercial printing in the region. Printing operations appeared not only in Holyoke (dubbed the "Paper City") and Springfield, but in many towns and villages in Western Massachusetts before the turn of the century. Newspapers, business forms, cards and stationery, invitations, and official public documents were printed on Kelly job presses, motorized Chandler and Price presses, Colt's Armory presses, and Kluge platen presses. When the fine arts printing movement began to flower following World War II, many of these presses, now replaced by modern offset equipment, could be acquired for bargain-basement prices, some even rediscovered in library and warehouse basements and given away for the "price" of removal. Some of the finest book artists in the country settled in the Valley, drawn perhaps by these favorable conditions, by the high concentration of poets and writers frequently teaching in the area, and by the magnetic presence of three superb artist-printers.

Harry Duncan, perhaps the most revered printer and publisher of American poetry in this country until his death in 1997, found his circuitous way from Grinnell College in Iowa to the Cummington School of the Arts in 1939. Cummington School, the brainchild of Katharine Frazier, a music professor at Smith College, drew to its rural acreage in West Cummington dozens of scholarship students in poetry, dance, music, painting, and sculpture. For a period of a dozen years it became a mecca for artists, some of whom achieved international recognition. Poets Allen Tate and Robert Lowell were two of its early luminaries, as was photographer Diane Arbus. Initially, Duncan arrived at Cummington on a poetry scholarship, but once there he found a handpress and some type, and with Frazier's encouragement, he learned to hand-set type and to design and print poetry chapbooks, books, and broadsides. Duncan's Cummington Press published the work of nearly a hundred poets, including William Carlos Williams, Wallace Stevens, Marianne Moore, Allen Tate, James Merrill, Robert Lowell, and Richard Wilbur. His elegant and spare designs, handsome typography, superb hand-printing, and use of laid paper made his books objects of value. Although he moved Cummington Press to Iowa City in 1956 and later to the University of Nebraska at Omaha (renaming it Abattoir Editions), the fifteen years in Cummington and in Rowe, Massachusetts, had resonances throughout the publishing and poetry worlds. A reserved man who believed that the "printed page was a window into the poem," Duncan saw the task of hand-setting type in a composing stick, then arranging and locking it inside the chase as if looking at it in a mirror, as the endlessly challenging joy of being a printer. Printers who set type by hand quote with obvious delight Duncan's most famous observation: "Setting type is the most intense form of reading there is — upside down and backwards."

Leonard Baskin, world-recognized sculptor, printmaker, watercolorist, and illustrator, reestablished his Gehenna Press (founded in 1942) in Northampton in the mid-1950s, shortly after he joined the art department at Smith College. While Baskin pursued his own art and oversaw designs for all sorts of projects at Gehenna, Harold McGrath, the man Barry Moser calls "the finest letterpress printer in America at the time," handled all of the printing chores. When Moser came to Northampton in 1962, he was introduced to Baskin, from whom he sought lessons in drawing. But when Moser turned to wood engraving, it was to McGrath he came to learn about pulling good proofs, typesetting, presses and printing, and limited-edition books. Later, in 1967, Moser and McGrath, with several others, founded a letterpress printing company, Hampshire Typothetae, which began to print limited-edition fine arts books for Moser's Pennyroyal Press as well as other presses around the country. In 1973 Carol J. Blinn learned the art of letterpress printing from Harold McGrath and, after spending a two-year apprenticeship at Gehenna, set up her own Warwick Press. Blinn remembers that Baskin was neither a pressman nor a mechanic, but rather a man of enormous erudition and imagination. McGrath was the pressman par excellence, she recalls, the man whose printing skill allowed Baskin to conceive increasingly complex and refined projects. Theirs was a printing partnership almost without parallel. Although both Baskin and McGrath died in 2000, their legacy lives in the work of many, many book artists in the Pioneer Valley and beyond.

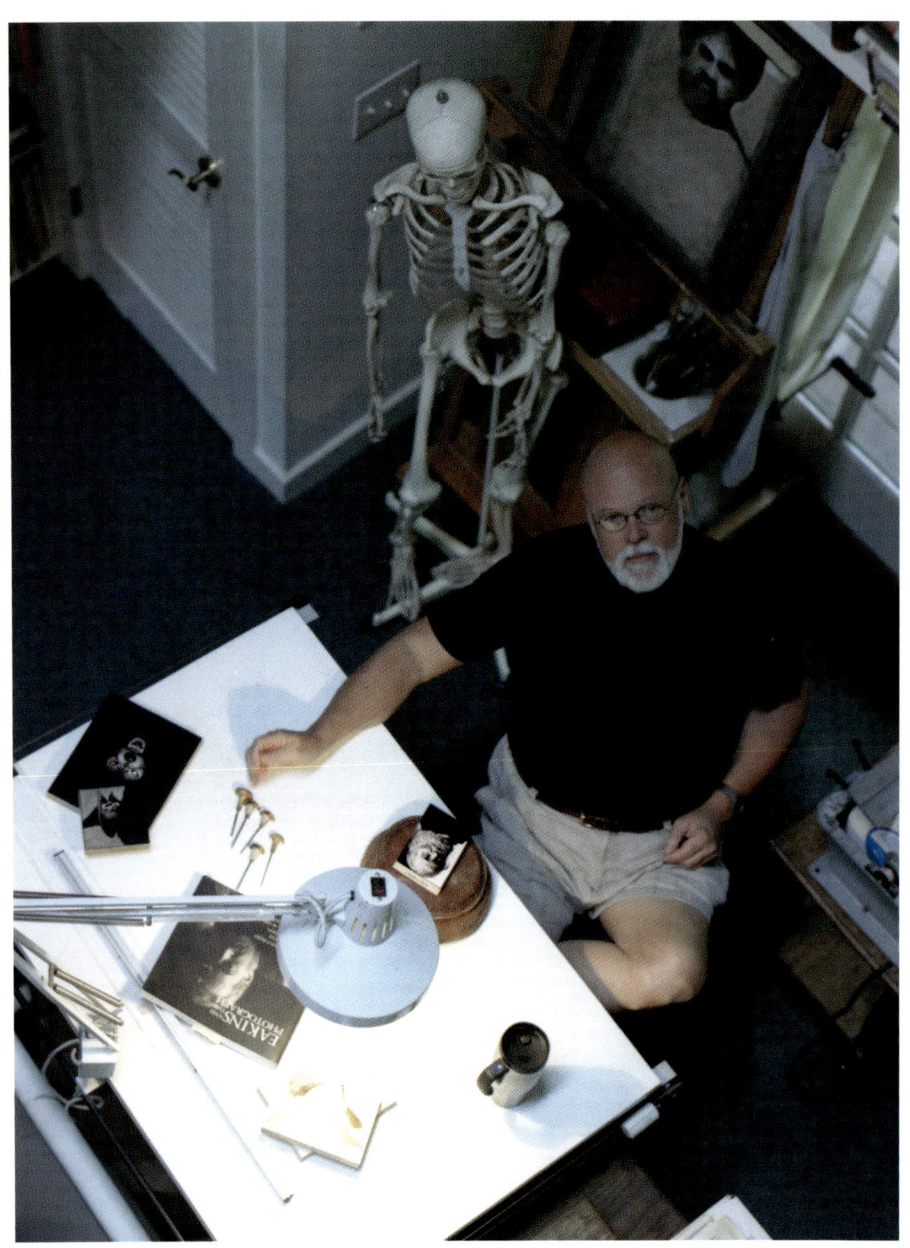

Barry Moser

BARRY MOSER

Engraver, Book Designer, Printer, Illustrator

T HE STEEP DRIVEWAY of Barry Moser's Hatfield home, the Rocks, climbs steadily through the series of switchback curves, each marked by a distinctive sign, garden container, or arrangement of rocks. Internationally known for his wood engravings, etchings, watercolors, and limited-edition books, Barry has won wide recognition and acclaim for his illustrations for *Moby-Dick*, *Adventures of Huckleberry Finn*, *Frankenstein*, *The Divine Comedy*, and particularly his 1999 edition of the King James Version of the Holy Bible.

Barry's two English mastiffs, Ike and Truman, massive fawn-colored dogs with inquistive faces and searching noses, meet me at the door. I recognize Truman immediately from the cover of the children's book, *Sit, Truman*, a story illustrated by Barry's watercolors and deemed "the absolute best picture book" by my niece's daughter, Sophie, who has good taste. Barry quickly appears and corrals the dogs into a skylighted area outside his work studio. We walk through a hallway studded with artwork — some striking photographs taken by Eudora Welty, which he points out; a large color print unmistakably the work of Leonard Baskin — through the kitchen of a serious cook, and to the dining room table. Almost instantly we are joined by Murray, a yellow "rescued cat" who will, Barry observes solemnly, soon be "telling his own story."

For anyone who has followed Barry's work and located his "signature"—a self-portrait in each book embedded among the other illustrations—the beard, the short, straight nose, the wire-rim glasses, the barrel chest all seem utterly familiar. His eyes are riveting: steady, bright, one might even say piercing. His hands are square, with tapered fingers and neatly trimmed nails, hands that belie the stress of high-speed drills, the pressure of the engraver, the wear and tear of the hundreds of scale models, drawings, inkings, and settings of type that have characterized his workdays for more than thirty years.

But it is Barry Moser's voice that most captivates. Well-modulated, floating at times on the cadences of the Tennessee Bible Belt "boy preacher" that he once was, sometimes opening into laughter, sometimes pulling back into intense *recitative*, it is a voice with heart, with guts. He'd make a great tenor in the Bach B Minor Mass.

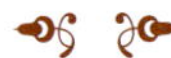

Barry was born in Chattanooga, Tennessee, in 1940. He attended military school (Baylor), Auburn University, and the University of Tennessee at Chattanooga, putting himself through his last two years of college as a licensed Methodist preacher. I already knew that he had taken a job teaching at Williston Academy in Easthampton, that he was subsequently introduced to master engraver Leonard Baskin and apprenticed with Harold McGrath at Baskin's Gehenna Press, and that he had largely taught himself the exacting art of wood engraving. But I did not know what precipitated his move to New England, or what had convinced him to stay.

"I came in 1967, and the clean way to answer your question is to say that I came to accept a teaching job at Williston Academy. But, of course, the answer is much more complicated than that. I had to escape the South, to expatriate myself from my people and from the society I was a part of.

"I don't mean to suggest anything self-glamorizing when I say I had to leave the South. I probably would not have moved here if I had the courage of my convictions. When the registration of black voters in Mississippi started, if I had gone and done what my conscience told me to do and if I had survived that experience, I'd probably still be in the South. And now, thirty years later, the South—the integrated South—is enormously attractive to me. I enjoy especially traveling into the Deep South, the Delta, Jackson, Mississippi. My first measurement of self is as a Southerner. I have that language. Of course I've cleansed myself of all the 'might could of's,' but then, up here, I began relearning my own language through reading Eudora Welty, Flannery O'Connor, Katherine Anne Porter. That language defines me.

"I was a boy preacher, licensed at nineteen and preaching for three years or so in a fairly fundamentalist series of churches. I was not as fundamentalist as the Jimmy Swaggarts of the world, but I had a deeply held belief that the Bible was the infallible word of God and that the passion, death, and resurrection of Christ was the salvation of humankind. But gradually I discovered that the people who were most likely to call themselves Christians were the least likely to actually be so. For example, I had a young woman in my Bible school class who got pregnant and was shunned. When I tried to offer my support to her, I lost my job, got fired—even though, as I recall, Jesus hung out with sorry sorts.

"But it wasn't just that form of hypocrisy. It went deeper. You know, as I get older I realize more and more that race is the defining issue of my life.

"I was brought up in a family of virulent racists. My grandfather and uncle were Klansmen—and those are simply the ones we *knew about*. Even when I attended a highly respected military school, Baylor, racism was rampant.

"In New England I found my spiritual home. Intellectual freedom is

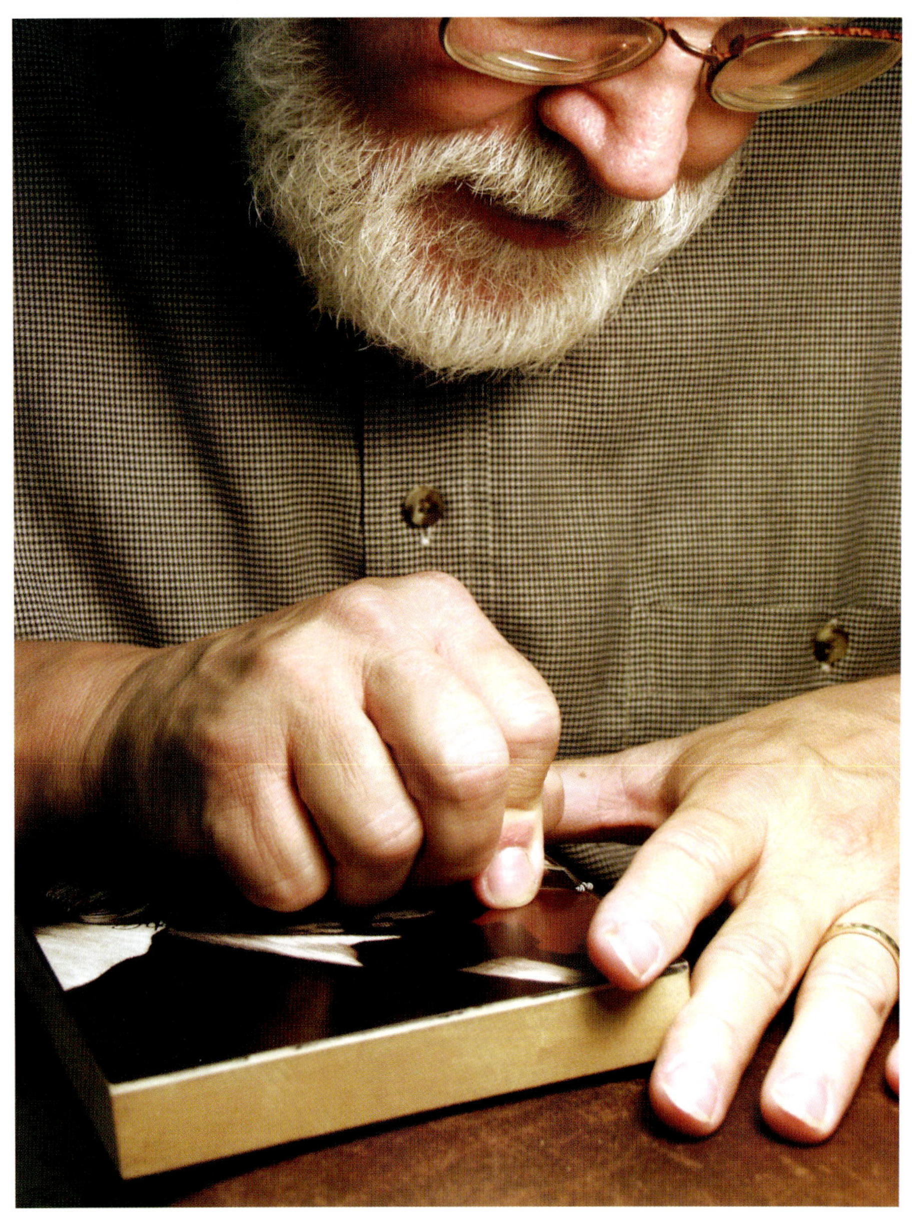

Engraving: "I can make anybody understand the process of wood engraving in an hour. But it takes years of persistence, years of work to perfect it."

the basis of that home, for with intellectual freedom I was left alone to think my own thoughts, to define my own values, a freedom I did not enjoy in the South at that time. Faulkner said something like 'religion in the South is like the air; it's the very element you breathe.' And Flannery O'Connor referred to the landscape of the South as 'Christ-haunted.'"

When I remark on how frequently Barry's illustrations pivot on haunted and haunting images—not only the interplay of shadows and light, but also terrifying images that are disturbing, yet compelling— he smiles as if he has heard that refrain before.

"I have a piece in the studio that I did when I was ten years old. Did you ever see the magazine ads for the Connecticut Famous Artists School? The one that advertises: DRAW ME! and then offers the model picture of a dog or a pretty woman's face?"

I nod in the affirmative.

"Well, I took that test and on the last page they give you a blank sheet where you are asked to show them what you like to draw. I did four or five drawings there: a man in tennis shoes, flexing his muscles, an airplane, the limb of a tree—and then a grotesque face. When I look at it now, I see that by the age of ten I was already involved with the subject matter of my adult world.

"I saw the Frankenstein movie as a boy and slept for many nights thereafter under my bed. And when I saw *Abbott and Costello Meet Frankenstein*, I discovered that the floor of the movie theater under the seats was sticky with dried Coca-Cola. I was terrified, and I also *enjoyed* those images. As a person I'm not dark in any way, shape, or form. But my imagination is dark. Dark and also leaning towards humor. There's no risk in staying solely near the light. And when you see the connections between dark and light and humor, it becomes easier to illustrate Melville, Dante, Homer, and Virgil."

Barry is well known for his use of contemporary figures as models for literary characters, sometimes producing great comic effects. In *The*

Wizard of Oz, for example, he chose to model the Wicked Witch of the West after Nancy Reagan, the Guardian of the Gate after Alexander Haig, and the disembodied head of the Wizard after Lee Iacocca. When he was doing his engravings for the Bible, he used Leonard Baskin as the model for Moses.

"Well," Barry interrupts, "Baskin wanted to be God, but he settled for Moses. I had thought I'd use him as Job, but he wouldn't agree to get naked for me.

"Unlike other people in my craft, I don't like to make up human faces. If I sit here and draw ten faces, even though they'll be different, they're all going to somehow look alike—some some stylistic connection. Even Doré's faces or Daumier's faces have that personal signature.

"I love the human face. That's my favorite subject, and I want ordinary human faces to appear even in—*especially in*—a text like the Bible. So that's why I used Donald Hall as Ecclesiastes (Ecclesiastes is a poet, you know), or Ezra Pound as the prophet Ezra, or Baskin, the master scuptor, as Moses—holding the chisel and mallet with which he hewed the two tables of stone. I work from real life and from photographic stills of real people playing fictional characters in movies and plays. Just recently I've been working on a portrait of Chaucer and one of Jane Austen. Nobody really knows what either looked like. We have 'likenesses,' but who knows how accurate they may be? I have a wall full of books of stills from movie and theater productions, and they're a great source for my imagination. I find a face, or three or four, a nose, a chin, and my imagination takes over."

Since 1985 Barry has designed and illustrated numerous children's books, including the award-winning *Jump Again! The Further Adventures of Br'er Rabbit, Appalachia, The Voices of Sleeping Birds,* and *When Birds Could Talk and Bats Could Sing.*

What differences does he see between illustrating classic texts and illustrating children's books? "Well, I confess that I used to think of the

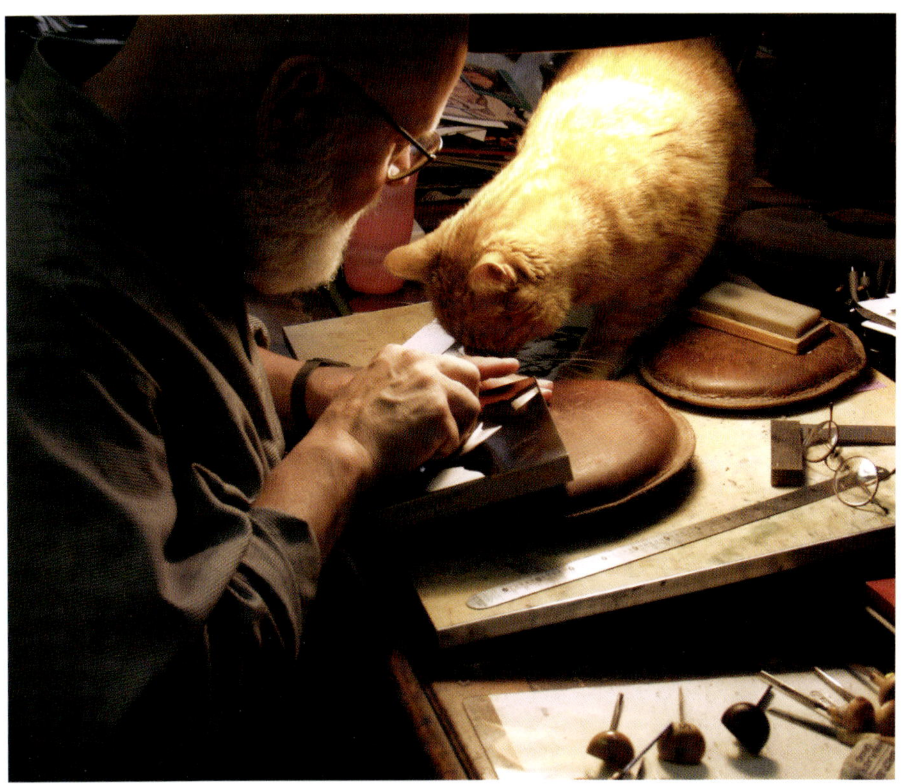

Work companions: Murray, the rescued cat, "will soon be telling his own story."

two as belonging to different classes of art. I remember saying to my partner, 'When I do my Bible (it was only a pipe dream then), I don't want them to say it was designed by an illustrator of children's books.' See how condescending I was? And then I discovered how *hard* it really is, since the pictures must also tell a story, must also carry their own narrative. You can't 'talk down' to children; they'll detect that in a moment. Instead, you have to say less, and that less must carry more. I admire children's authors and illustrators, and being surrounded by so many superb ones right here in the Valley is another stimulation."

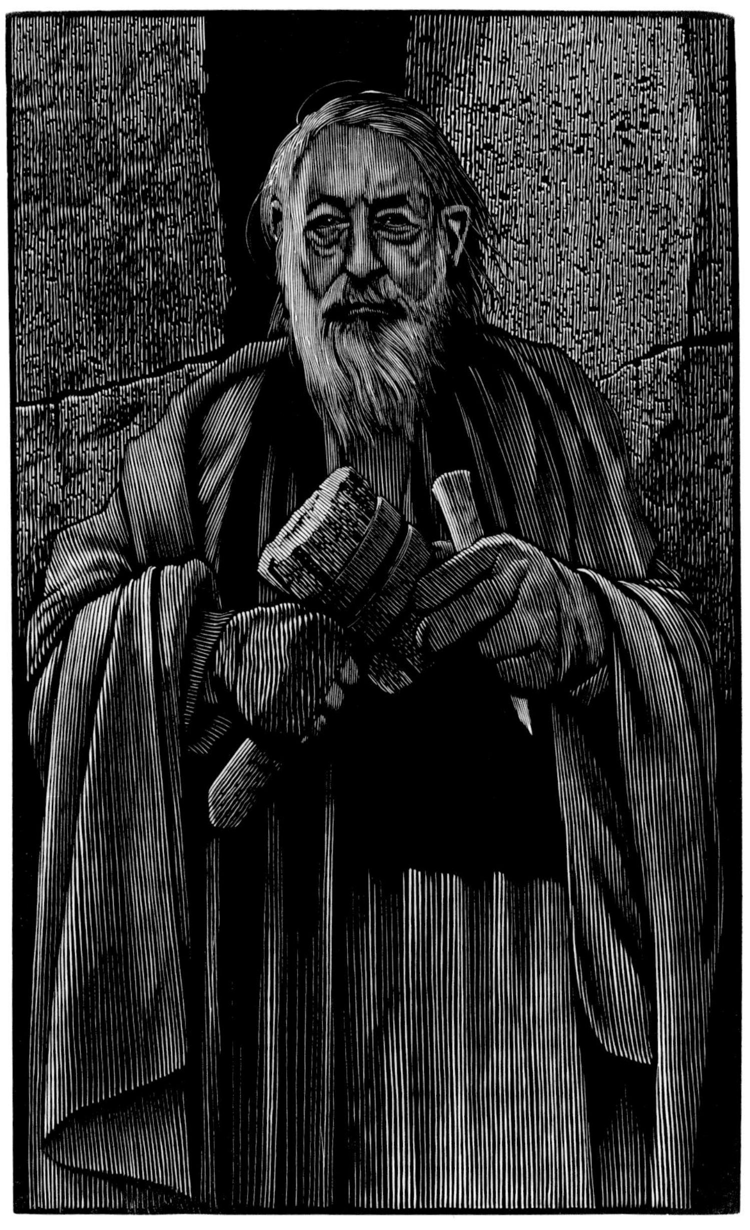

From the Pennyroyal Caxton Bible, a relief engraving of Moses, hewing the tablets of stone, modeled on sculptor Leonard Baskin. Barry engraves his images on material called Resingrave that simulates the boxwood blocks he once used, which are no longer available.

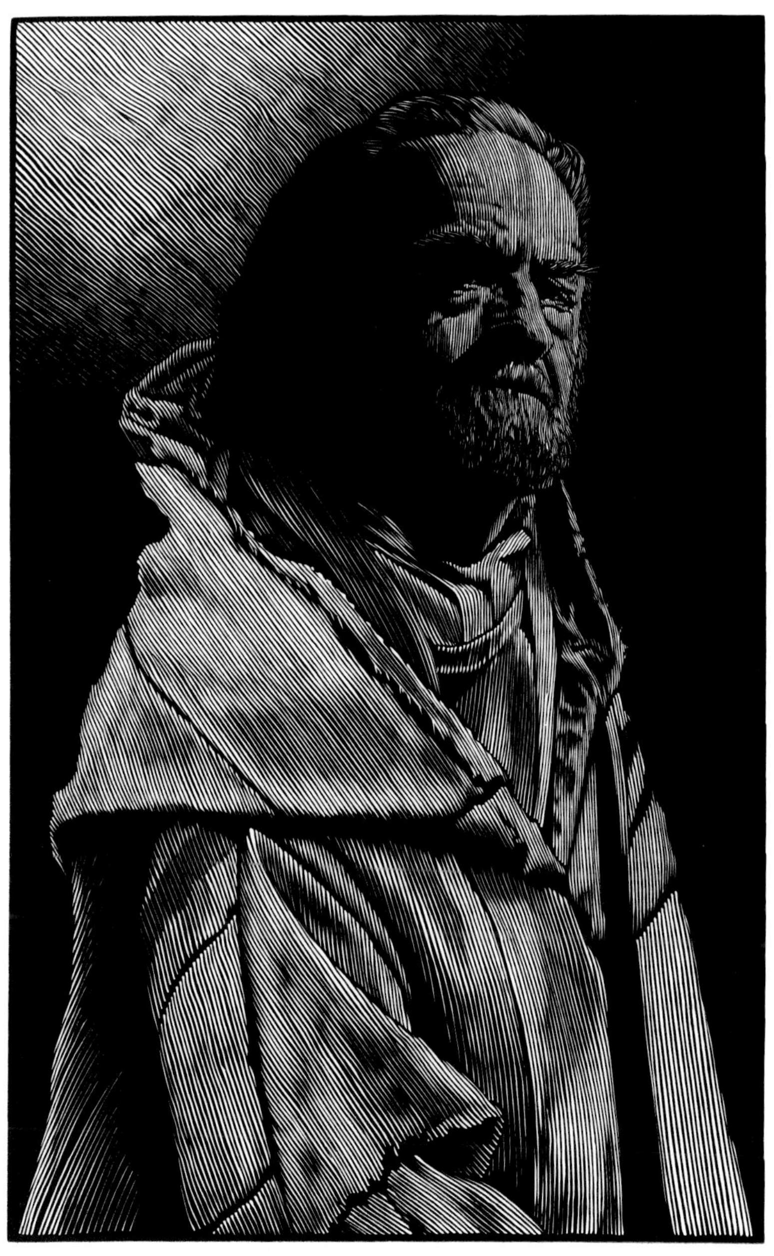

Relief engraving of Ecclesiastes, from the Pennyroyal Caxton Bible.
Barry modeled this image of the preacher and poet on
the poet Donald Hall.

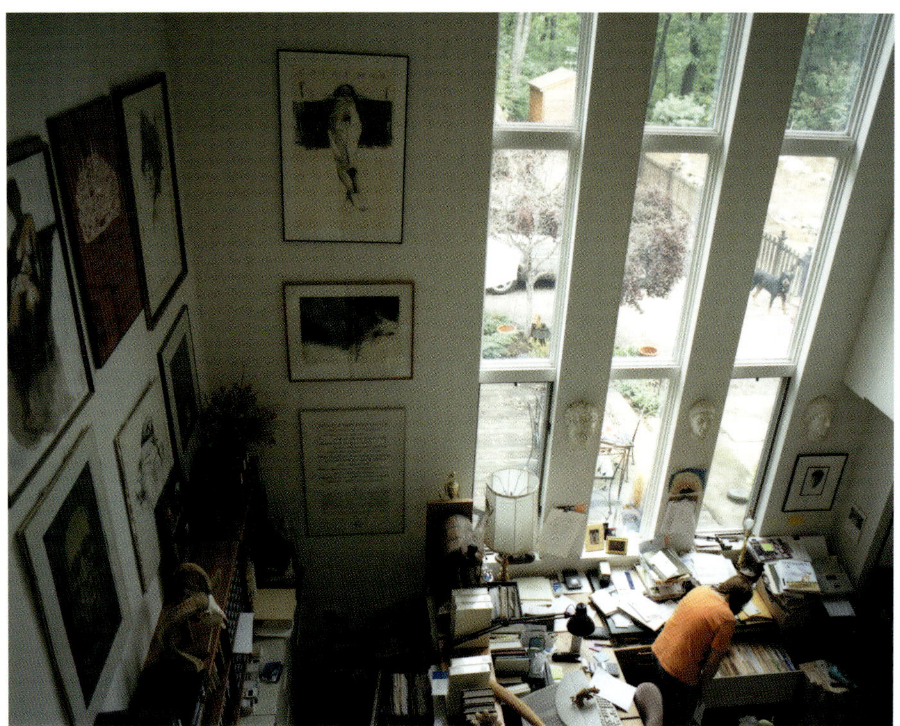

The high-ceilinged studio space, suffused with light

In 1999, after four exhausting years of work, Barry Moser published the Pennyroyal Caxton Bible, becoming the first artist to design and illustrate the Bible alone since Gustave Doré did so in 1865. Superlatives began to flow: "world-class designer," "wood engraver without peer," virtuoso illustrator."

I wondered whether such superlatives complicate the question of what's next, whether they put you in competition with yourself.

"Oh, no. Not really. When somebody like Simon Brett, whom I consider to be the greatest living engraver today, offers praise, then that is bolstering, that gives energy to the work. But the rest of it is horseshit.

That kind of inflated praise is just poppycock. The comments that stick are either comments from those who are in a position to know, or from those who have the courage to be more critical. Negative reviews are more instructive, don't you think? They're the ones you remember.

"What really complicates 'what's next' for me is the sorry state of book publishing in today's market. The industry is no longer a force in forging American literary taste. It's losing its courage, its guts, and is kowtowing to the 'taste' of Barnes & Noble, Borders, Amazon. I have many projects I'd like to do—Chaucer's *Canterbury Tales*, an illustrated complete Shakespeare, *The Lord of the Rings*. I'd love to do *Paradise Lost* — but who will take that chance, put up the money—." His voice trails off.

"Let's go into the studio," he says, beckoning. Back along the hallway, past Truman and Ike, the organized, well-lighted space where Barry works opens invitingly. Walls rising to an open balcony are covered with artwork, citations and awards, and rows and rows of shelved books. Sitting next to me at an ink-stained desk, slowly, meticulously, in the manner of an experienced and patient teacher, he explains the process he uses to produce a wood engraving. He confesses that his first attempt at wood engraving—one cut in a slab of redwood with an X-Acto knife—was a "sorry thing." But after he located the proper wood blocks and engraving tools, and particularly after he found Harold McGrath at Gehenna Press, who would print his wood engravings, he began to move into a medium of expression he could call his own.

"Woodcuts are made in the plain grains," he explains, "but wood engravings are cut in the end grain. Wood engraving blocks are constructed out of very dense wood. Boxwood is ideal, but because of its scarcity and almost prohibitive cost, many engravers—including myself—had to stop some years ago because we could neither find nor afford it.

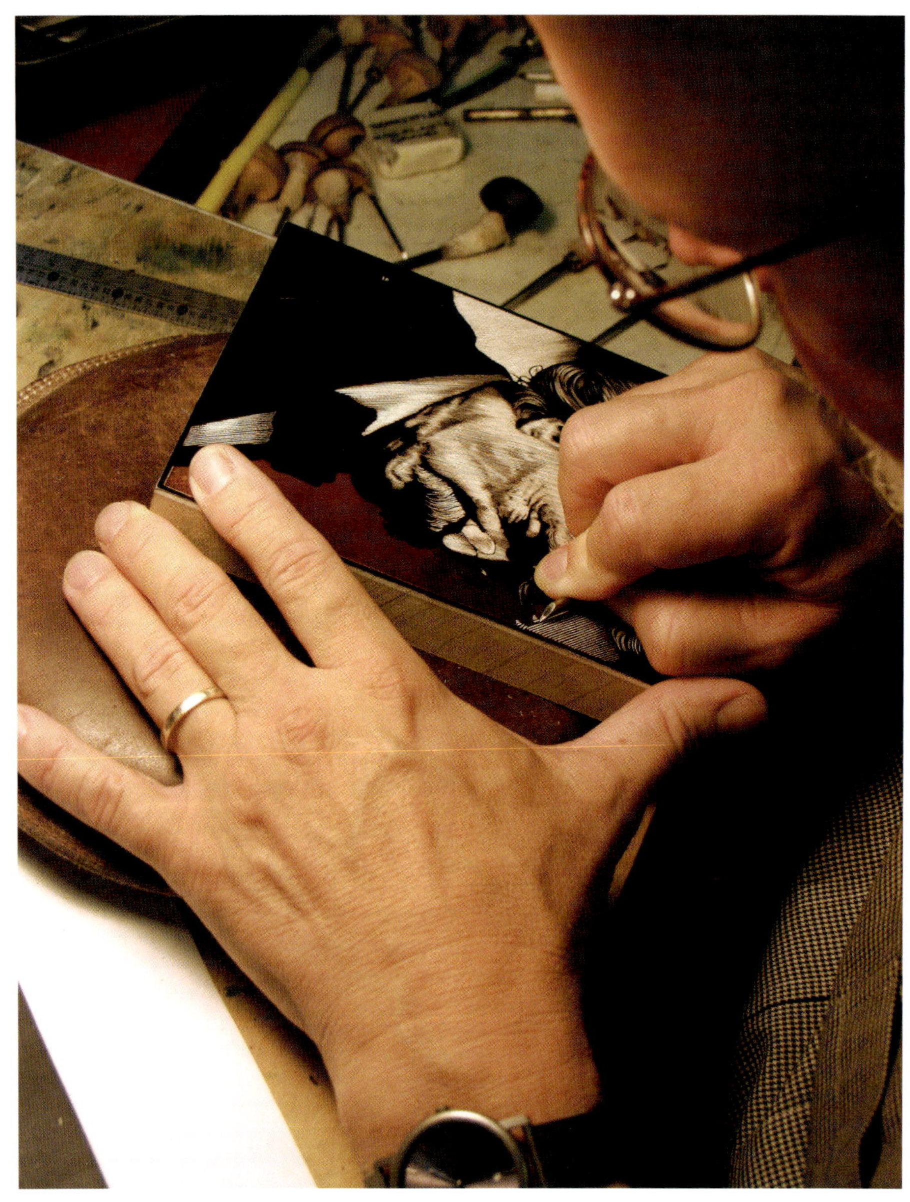

Muscle memory: "Ultimately, it is the muscles of the forearms and hands that 'understand' the art."

"Fortunately, about the time I ran out of wood, Kim Merker [founder of the Windhover Press] at the University of Iowa, sent me a piece of particleboard with a plastic surface, a 'wood engraving substitute.' The material was invented by Richard Woodman and he called it Resingrave, an epoxy polymer cast on medium-density particleboard. At first I was highly skeptical. It didn't smell like wood, it didn't look like wood, surely it wouldn't cut like wood. But once I tried to work with it, once I felt its suppleness, I became a convert."

"It looks really complicated," I say, looking at the intricate cuts on the block he has on his desk.

"I can make anybody understand the process of wood engraving in a hour. But it takes years of persistence, years of work to perfect it. Ultimately, it is the muscles of the forearms and hands that 'understand' the art. Muscle memory produces the particulars, leaving the mind free to invent." He pulls my chair a bit closer to the desk.

"I transfer the drawn image onto the block. I tone the block's surface to a color darker than that of the wood itself. This allows me to see the engraved line as white against a dark background as I engrave it— precisely the way it will print. I use a warm brown color of printing ink as a toner.

"Then I engrave the block on top of these leather engraver's bags." I notice he has two leather bags, one on top of the other, which are stitched all around except for a one-inch open section through which a heavy filler like sand or BBs can be inserted. These pliable bags allow him to turn or manipulate the block while he is making the cuts.

Barry demonstrates several of the engraving tools he uses as well as the several ways he holds them, each tool and each position producing a different kind of cut. He swivels in his chair, looks me directly in the eyes, and says, a smile playing at the corners of his mouth, "It's really quite simple."

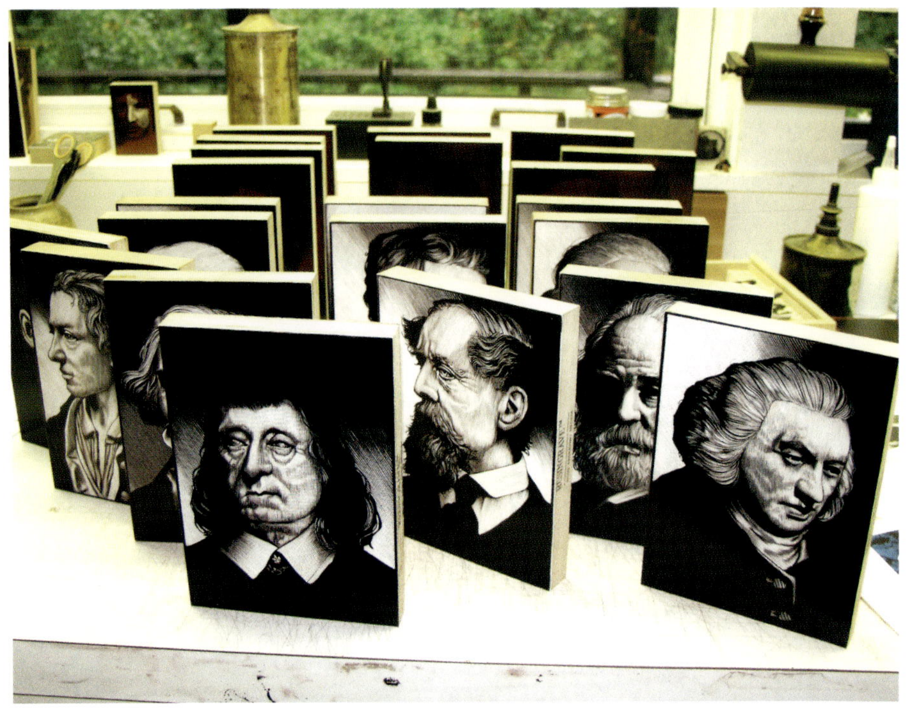

The faces of literary genius: "I love the human face. I never tire of working on it."

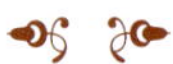

Throughout our conversation wonderful Mozart CDs have been playing. When I remark that I read somewhere that as he was doing the illustrations for the Bible he listened again and again to the Mozart
Requiem, he smiles and says, "Oh yes, the Requiem—and Monteverdi,
and Palestrina, all that glorious music of the church. I'm fascinated by
people like Mozart because he seems like me, a reprobate. When I came
to do the Bible, I did not engage it as the infallible word of God, but
rather as sacred literature, read and respected by an ordinary man, a
profane man, an apostate. Remember what Mozart said to Joseph II (at

least in Peter Schaffer's *Amadeus*), who was worried about his questionable behavior?

"Your Grace, it is true that I am a profane man, but I assure you, sire, my work is not."

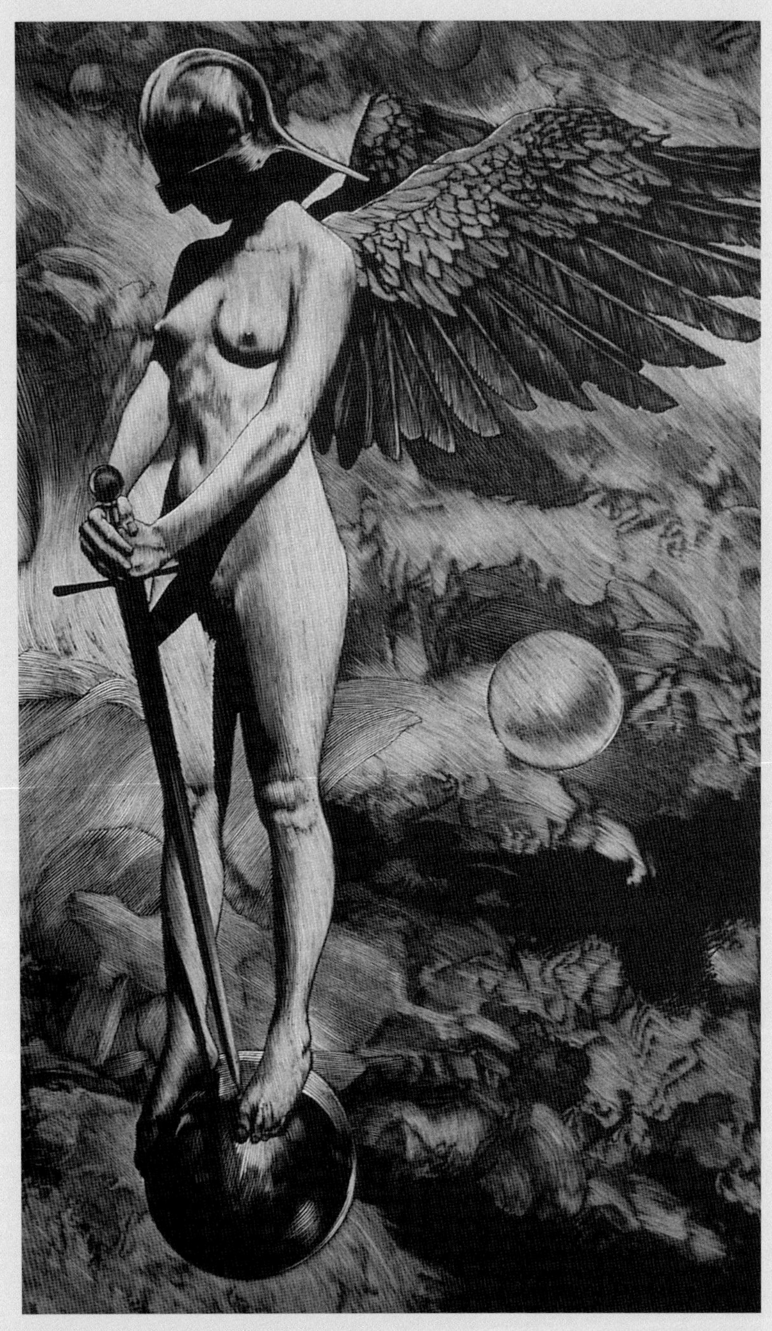

"WHEN HE PREPARED THE HEAVENS, I WAS THERE"

Relief engraving, 29" × 17"

"Wood engravings and relief engravings are, by their very nature, intimate objects. Wood engraving was invented as an illustration medium for books, and as such the scale is usually small. Part of the challenge of this engraving, whose dimensions are 29 by 17 inches, is its size; it and another, the 'Last Judgment,' that I made for the Bible, may be the largest engravings ever made that were invented, drawn, and engraved by the same hand. To be sure, there are larger ones, but they were engraved by craftsmen other than the artist who invented and drew the image. Winslow Homer's large engravings illustrating scenes from the battlefields of the American Civil War are a case in point.

"The image is Wisdom. She is found in the eighth chapter of Proverbs where she says, 'When he prepared the heavens, I was there.' This figure of Wisdom, the text says, is a woman, and that intrigues me greatly. Being the iconoclast that I am, I rather like the idea of the Godhead being quadripartite: God, the Father, the Son, the Sanctus Spiritus, and—Sophia, Wisdom. I mean, what else, if she was there with God when he prepared the heavens, 'set up from everlasting, from the beginning, or ever the earth was.' Don't you find that intriguing?"

—Barry Moser

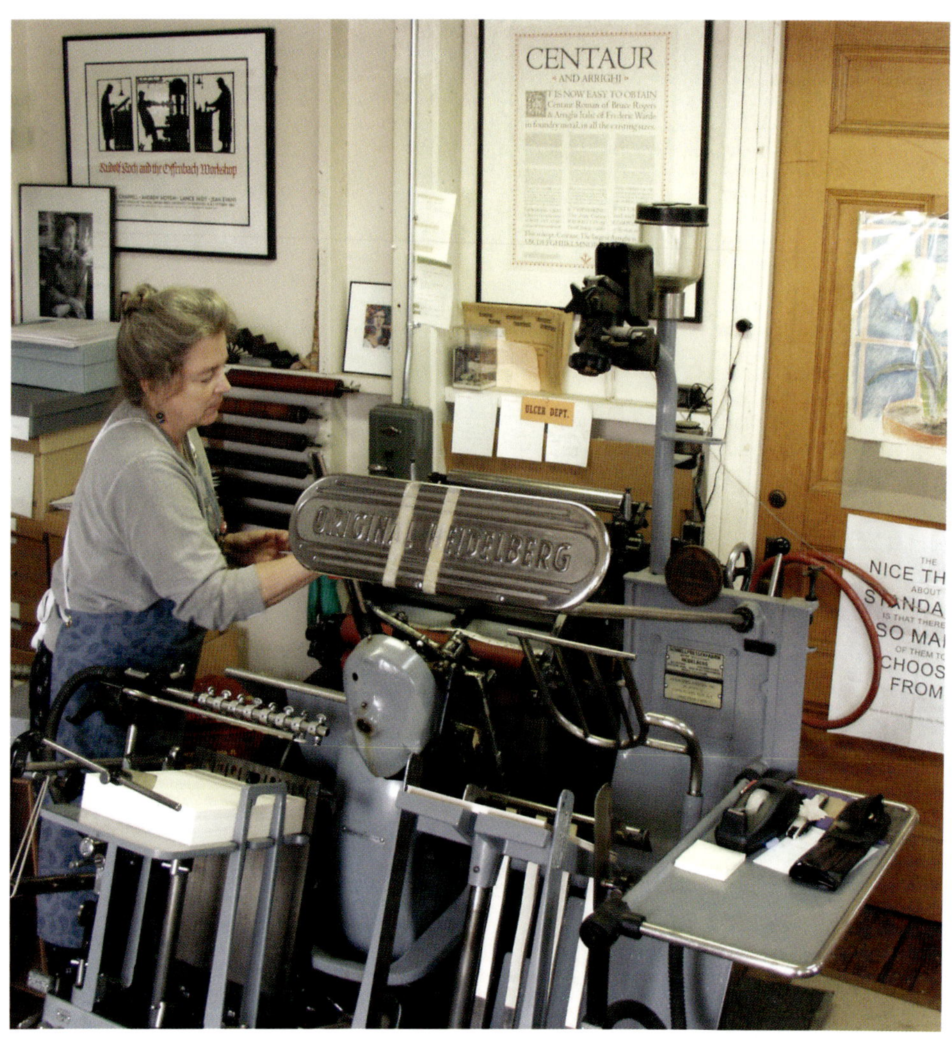

Carol J. Blinn

CAROL J. BLINN

Printer, Designer, Paper Decorator, Binder

ONE COTTAGE STREET, a red-brick former factory overlooking Nashawannuck Pond in Easthampton, is home to a diverse group of Pioneer Valley artists. Weavers and quilters, woodworkers, painters, and potters have carved out studio space in the refurbished building; Carol Blinn's printing shop, conveniently situated next to a large freight elevator, occupies a large high-ceilinged space on the third floor. For thirty years now, under the imprimatur of Warwick Press, Carol has turned out stunning limited editions of poetry and prose, broadsides, stationery, bookplates, bookmarks, cards, and invitations. As her interest in all facets of book production grew, she learned not only to design books, broadsides, and invitations that are beautifully proportioned and arranged on the page, but also to bind books, to create colorful and visually interesting covers and endpapers, and to add her own distinctive illustrations to a text. Even within the richly layered book arts community in the Pioneer Valley, it's rare to find someone who has mastered all of the skills required to make a complete book. Artists specialize: They design, they print, they bind, they write, or they illustrate. Carol does it all, and seemingly with equal enthusiasm, dexterity, and vision.

Carol is bidding good-bye to another printer friend as I climb the last flight of stairs to her shop. At first glance, she appears small,

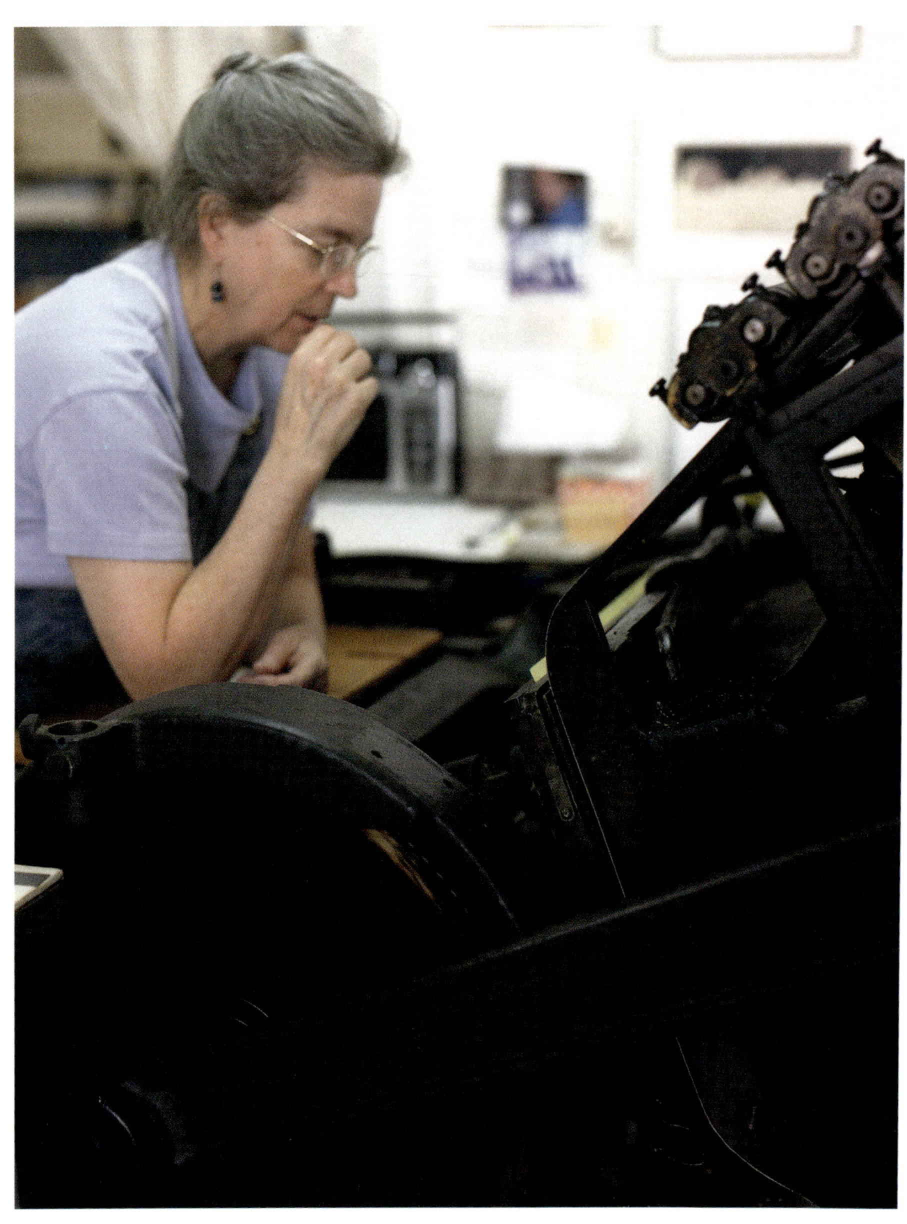

At the Kluge press. "I love that this press is just my age."

slighter than the printer in my mind's eye, the one who can manipulate a heavy Kluge platen press, tighten and oil its parts, set an entire page of lead type and lock it in with quoins and keys. But she moves with authority around the three presses she shows in quick succession. Obligingly, she starts up the Heidelberg press to demonstrate how the air suction paper feeder works and, more impressively, how the sheet moves in one elongated graceful sweep from feeder to ink to impress to printed page.

"When I work at this press," she said, spreading her feet a bit and squaring her body up to the formidable front of the machine, "I am careful always to wear a peaked baseball cap and to tie my hair back or tuck it under the cap." She touches the back of her long ponytail, as if to demonstrate. "Even after years and years of printing I must always remind myself not to lean in too far, to always be careful. And you never, never reach in."

The way she touches the cylinder of the Heidelberg gently with a cloth, wiping away excess oil, and the way she speaks of tightening a press with care rather than brute strength, suggest that success in working with well-worn machines dating from the 1940s depends far less on strength than on finesse. And on experience.

The press area of the shop is in the back, and as we thread our way up to the front table, she points out various workstations where she does design, illustrations, bookbinding, paper decoration. The shop is filled with makeready tables, type cases, glass-doored bookshelves, and upright shelves with dozens of cubbyholes, each one filled with colorful and textured papers. The net effect is of controlled chaos; Carol appears to know exactly where everything is.

"When I was first learning bookbinding from Arno Werner [master bookbinder for Gehenna Press]," she explains, "he showed me how to make pastepaper, that is, how to use paste to make an intricate combed pattern on the page. I was hooked. Subsequently, I've tried my

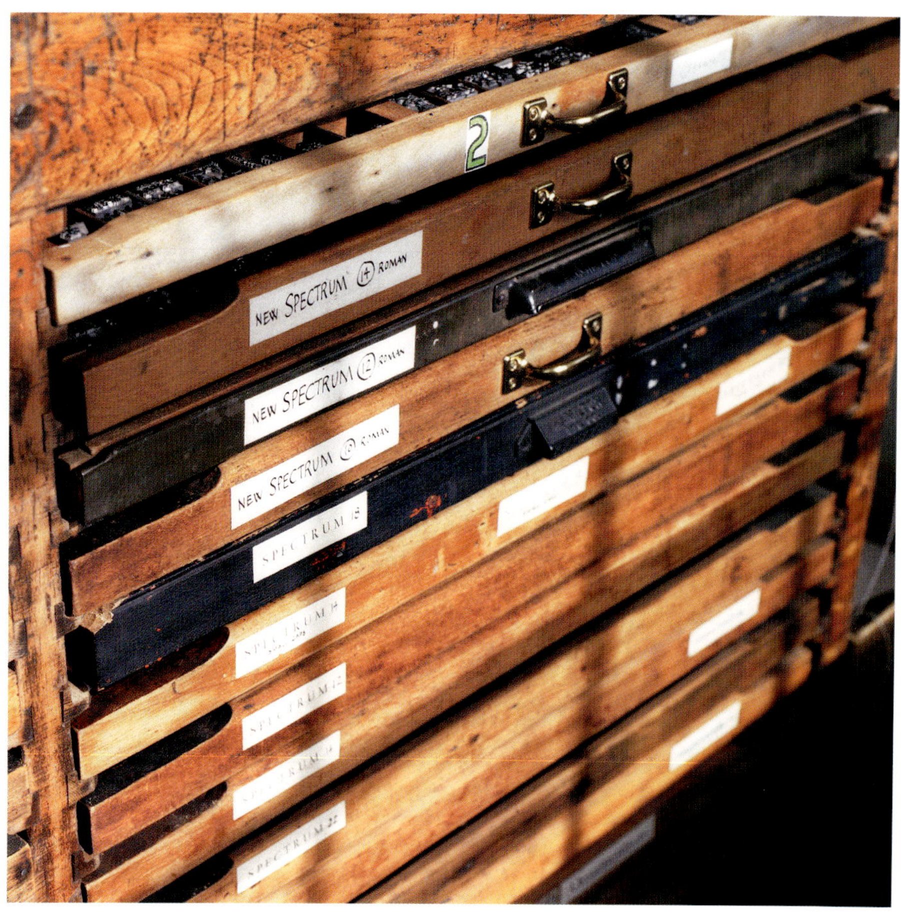

Drawers of type cataloged by font (the style of the typeface) and by point size (the height and width of the letters). A letterpress printer often sets thousands of metal letters to make up a single page of a book.

hand at marbling, suminagashi, and stenciling. Each method of decorating paper has its own appeal. I study the special demands of each project before deciding which one to choose."

She smiles, a distinct dimple deepening in one cheek. "Don't you

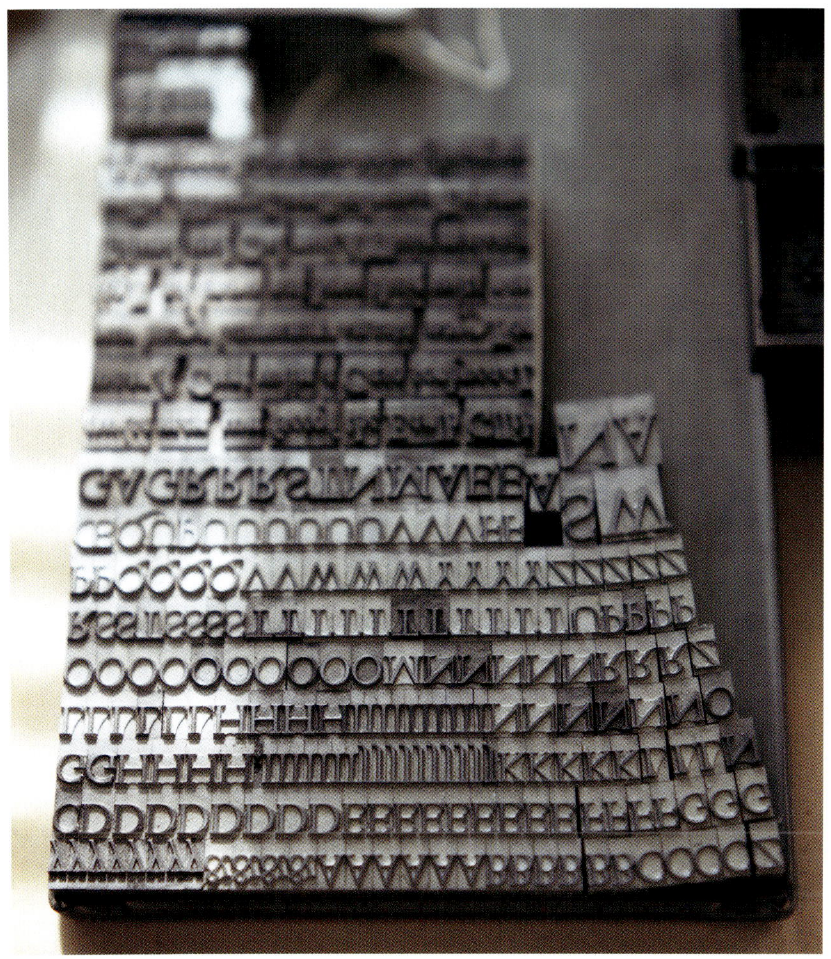

Movable type

just love the *stuff*? I think that is the first thing that appealed to me
when I turned in the direction of art. I loved the supplies—all of them.
And here I can play with tools and papers, oil cans and screwdrivers,
paintbrushes, inks, acrylic paints, oils, watercolors, machinery built in

the forties that can be fixed with a wrench. I can choose individual letters made of lead that can be set and manipulated and ultimately printed on a press, linen thread covered with beeswax that I sew by hand into signatures of printed papers, and"—she takes a deep breath—"I can use the most important tools of all: eye-hand coordination and a vision in my mind.

"I think I came to my love of tools quite early. My early education in spackling wallboard, birdhouse building, and table saw use came at my father's side. But my mother had her own set of tools, kept in a special box, and from her I learned much about the value of using and caring for tools of one's own. She had gone to a fashion design school, was an expert at sewing, and before entering kindergarten I knew how to sew clothes for my dolls, how to bake bread and cookies, how to make greeting cards and paper dolls.

"My mother was also a lover of the outdoors, and my brother and I were treated to nature walks. We studied small animals, insects, seashells, trees, rocks, and particularly we fed and watched all kinds of birds. That influence lasted a very long time, for when I began to do illustrations for some of my own books, I noticed that ducks tended to find their way in repeatedly. My parents had given me two nifty Pekin ducklings when I was young; how did I know they would become my totem?"

I asked Carol if she had always known she wanted to be an artist.

"Well, not exactly. What I dreamt of most in my young life was becoming a doctor. But my first experience with a biochemistry course at Clark University convinced me that dream was dashed. The next semester I moved my sights over to taking art history and studio art courses at the Worcester Art Museum, and I felt instantly at home.

"After I graduated, I worked in trade publishing at Barre Publishers, a place where I met and worked with some of the best book designers in the country, freelancers all. Sadly, my days ended at Barre when our president died quite suddenly. We were bought out by Crown Publishers and I was without a job. Several months later, via a circuitous route, I ended up at the Gehenna Press (which I located by going through the Yellow Pages under 'printers'). In July of 1973 I walked into 15 Clarke Avenue in Northampton, where I met Leonard Baskin and Harold McGrath. By August I was learning to set type by hand and printed my first piece of work, a sonnet by Shakespeare, on a platen press. I fell in love with everything about the place. Even the people."

Leonard Baskin was widely known to have exacting standards and perhaps some impatience with beginners. I wondered how they got along.

Slowly she nodded, then smiled a kind of conspiratorial smile.

"Actually I was allowed to be at Gehenna because Harold McGrath was willing to teach me how to print. Simple as that. He ran the day-to-day operations while Leonard Baskin came by periodically to attend to projects in the works. I had no notion of how famous Leonard really was, but I came to regard him with some measure of fear and awe as I got to know him. He often scared the bejeezus out of me. But I once did stand up to his fierce temper, and after that episode we got along quite well. I think it was my lack of backbone and my own sense of inadequacy that Leonard at first seized on with a vulture's eye for the newly dead. I was timid. And Leonard was so sure. Of everything. He was probably the most brilliant man I have ever—or will ever—meet in my life. And I grew to have great affection for him coupled with feelings of wonder at the powerful work he produced in many mediums.

"But then there was Harold, with whom I worked each day and whom I adored. He seemed to return the affection. His self-effacing manner made even the most wretched apprentice feel that, well, yes, Harold had bungled jobs *much* worse than any apprentice had. He was a consummate teacher who filled the pressroom with laughter and silliness. He took great pride in my being able to run the 'big press' (a

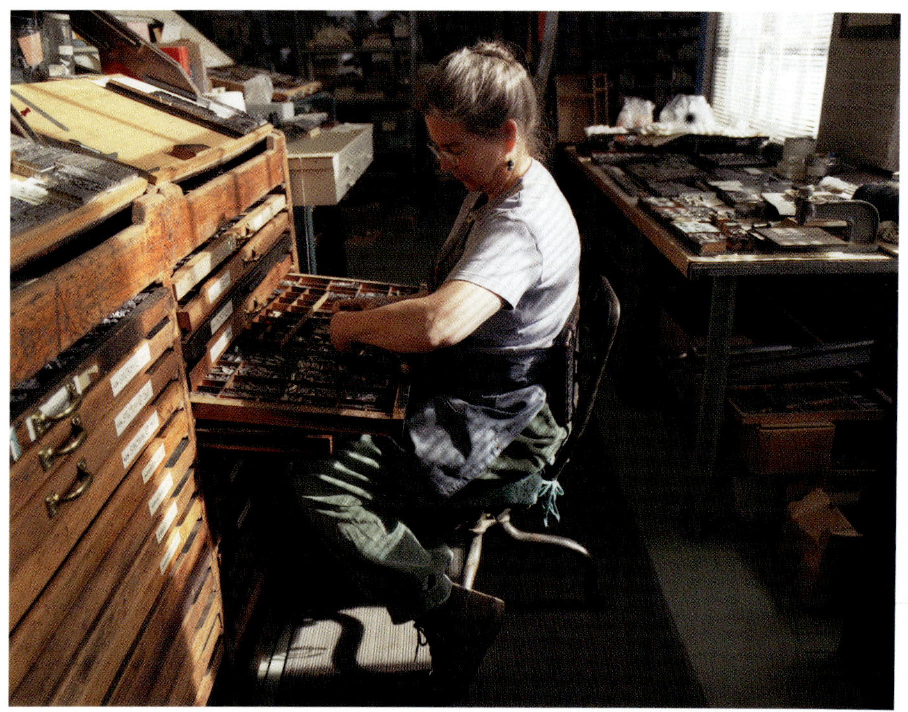

Setting type in a composing stick: "The most intense form of reading there is: upside down and backwards."

25-by-38-inch automatic sheet-fed Kelly) when we did big books and large prints.

"It was through Harold that I was introduced to Arno Werner, the man who bound most of Gehenna's editions for many years. Harold drove me up to Arno's place in Pittsfield that first autumn of my apprenticeship. Arno had a nifty shop that smelled of cigar ash, moldy binder's board, hide glue, and cat hair. He taught me how to bind my first edition of books and started my lifelong love affair with decorated paper. We would start a project and work until we dropped, pausing

The WRITER, *the* MADMAN *& the* PRINTER

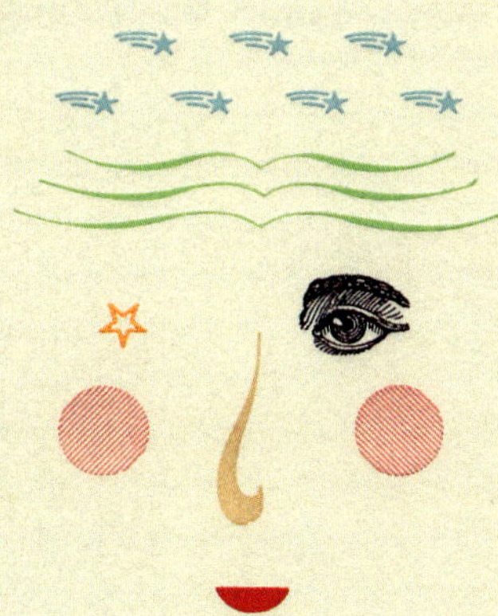

Notes on a Writer's Artistic License,
Or, Setting the Record Straight

Simon Winchester & Carol J. Blinn

WARWICK PRESS

Easthampton 2 0 0 2 Massachusetts

Front page of The Writer, The Madman, & The Printer: *"I keep trying to match the colors, images, drawings, and paper to the images I carry inside my head."*

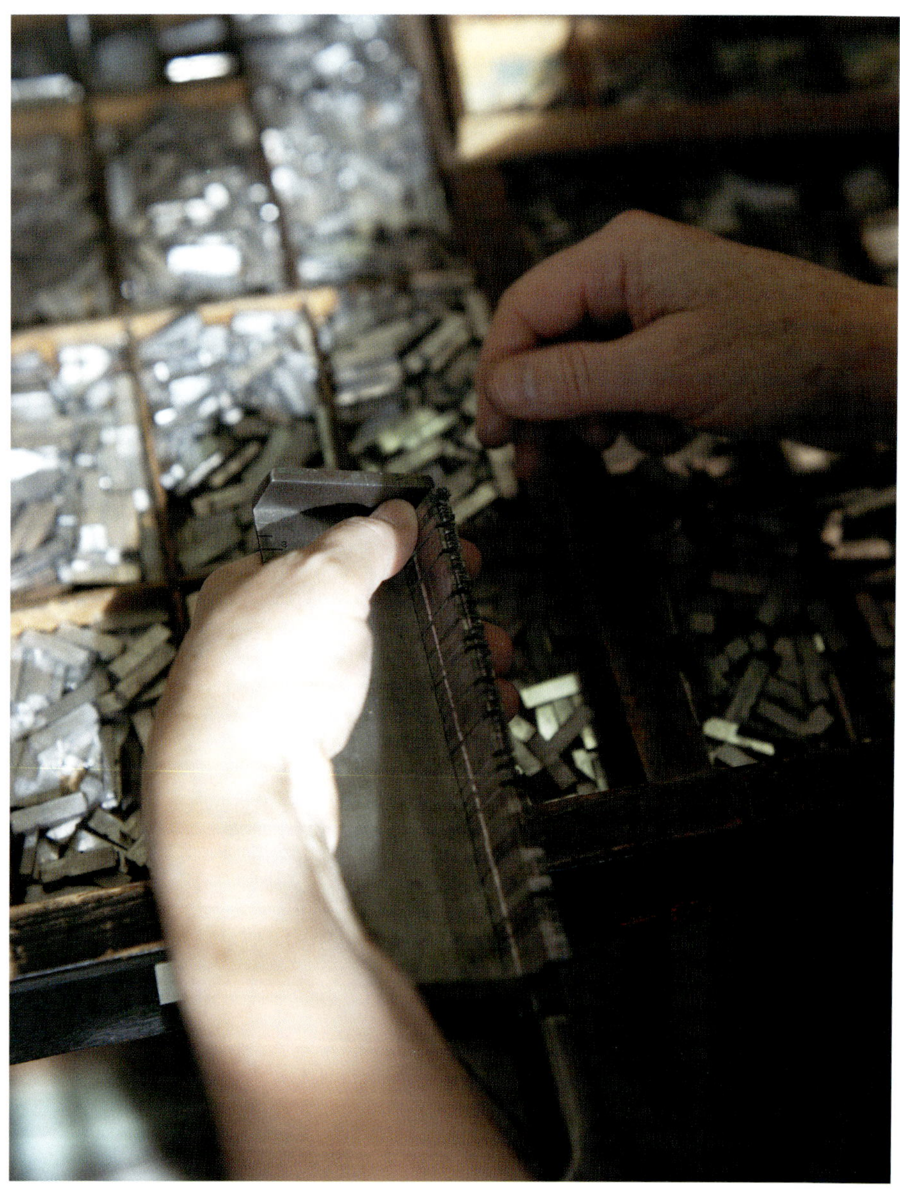

Each line of type is hand-set, aligned, properly spaced, and locked into a chase with quoins and keys. The raised letters and images, when pressed onto paper, leave an imprint, an impression missing in offset printing.

only for tea and lunch breaks, then suppers of spaghetti and salad, then back to the shop for more work. He was never stingy with his materials (some of which I later realized were very expensive) or with his time. Step by step he taught me the complexities of making a well-bound book by hand. I have yet to achieve the grace he had at the height of his powers, but I keep trying."

I asked Carol if she had a favorite project, a watershed project, from her thirty years of printing—perhaps one of the books bought by the Library of Congress or the British Museum?

She takes book after exquisite book from a neat stack on her work-table, handing each one over lovingly, as if to say, "My favorite is the one I am working on now." Among these is a book called *The Dial Painters,* a group of poems by John Barr that explores the lives of the women who fashioned the tips of brushes used to paint the luminous dots on clock and watch faces. Their exposure to the luminous paint left them with radium poisoning, and Carol has replicated the tiny luminous dots of their lethal art on the title page. We examine together a booklet ti-tled *Two by Two,* poems that celebrate the occasion of a joint reading by Donald Hall and Richard Wilbur, brought together by the invitation of Jack Kelleher in June of 2000 in the Village Church in Cummington, Massachusetts. Carol's book catches—in its creamy parchment wrap-per and the two-color ghosts of horses galloping underneath—some visual equivalent of the long friendship of two of America's premier poets and traces of the images in their poetry that linger in the mind and heart.

"I keep trying to match the colors, images, drawings, and paper to the images I carry inside my head. As I grow older, I begin to recog-nize that there is a thread of sensibility that runs throughout my work. I did not set out to develop a style nor did I ever consciously feel it was important. But over time, I have watched my design sense and my use of type gather strength and grow to a point where I do have a recognizable style. I must admit I like that. I also like knowing that, as others have told me, my work can please, can give delight. I know it has inspired some students to work in the book arts. And that is a quietly wonderful and humbling realization."

Busy curating an invitational exhibit at Union College in Schenectady, New York, Carol was finishing up invitations to fifty-four female printers when we spoke. The exhibit, held in August 2003, showcased the wide variety of professional work done by a multitude of women printers; Carol was also interested in celebrating the personal stories of women who are drawn to printing, to mastering the running of a reluctant press, to learning the art of bookbinding. After three decades in letterpress publishing, she continues to believe fervently in the work. Yet, given all the time, the care, the expensive materials, I had to ask her how she keeps her operation afloat.

"I'm not always sure, from moment to moment, that I am afloat. For years I've maintained a commercial side of the business, printing invitations, stationery, bookplates, bookmarks, and paper ephemera to help pay the rent and offset some of the costs of printing limited-edition books. It's never been easy, and particularly now that we have classic typefaces available and formatted for computer use, what I do, from a cost-effective standpoint, grows harder and harder. The new technology is beneficial in many ways. But it's not where my heart is. Sitting in front of a computer screen for hours on end would send me to the nuthouse. I need to set my hands to work in concert with my brain. It's that tactile connection with all my *stuff* that I can't imagine being without. When it's all going well, I absolutely lose myself in the work. It's the *act of doing* that attracts me."

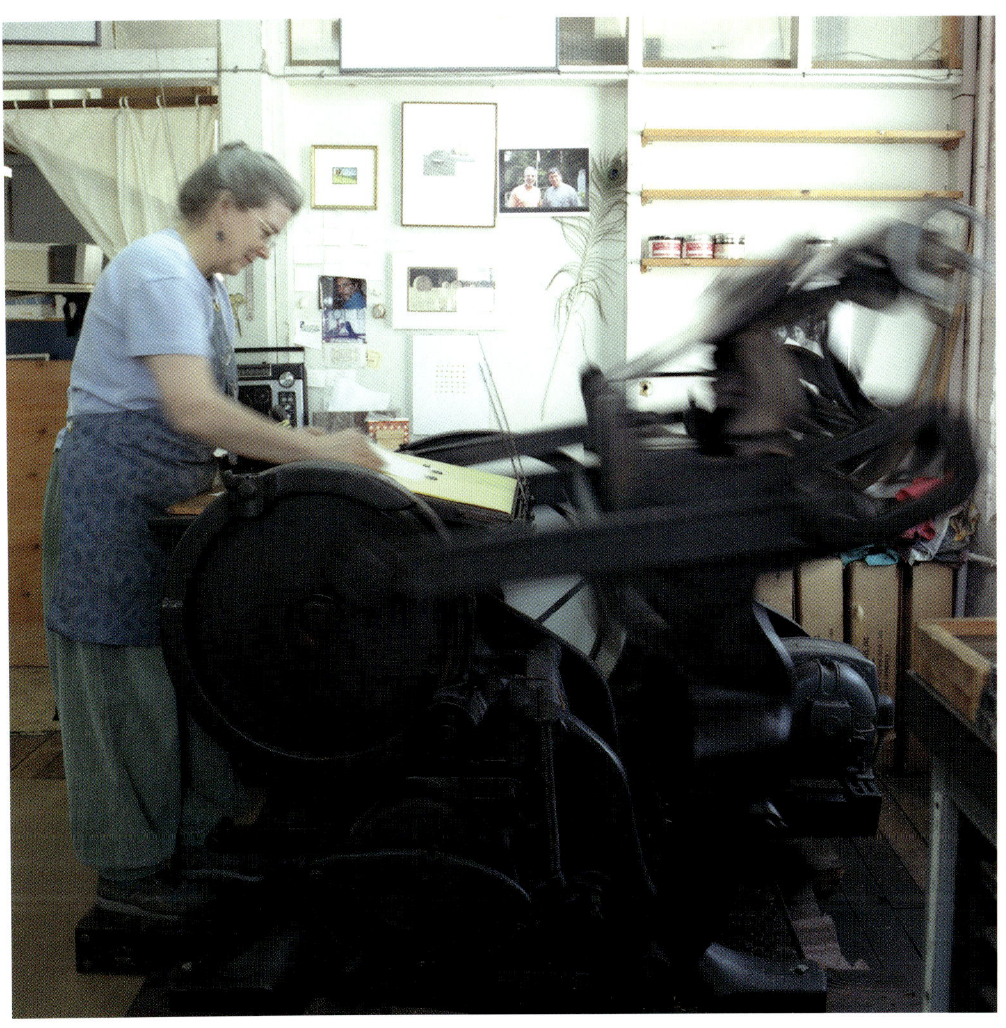

Working on the Kluge. Recently Carol curated an exhibit at Union College show-casing the works of female printers, titled "Girl Printers Strut Their Stuff."

DUCK ~~POULTRY~~ POETRY
^
(OR, ONCE UPON A TIME/BOOK EIGHT)

5"×7½"; 19 pages; letterpress printed; type, Monotype Gill Sans; handmade, hand-colored Fabriano paper wrapper; sewn binding made with goat vellum tapes laced through the covers

"Why have I singled out this book for special notice? Perhaps because it is my newest and I fall in love with each new book in the making of it. Or it might be because in my middle age I am making an unapologetic move into using my ducks as metaphors to describe the human experience. It might be because I have, for many years, wanted to make a book with illustrations using watercolored pastel colors with colored inks on the line drawings. It might be because of my need to make another non-adhesive binding using goat vellum tapes. Or it might be because Frieda Fitzenmeyer, my alter ego, wanted to spread her wings and write poems describing simple scenes and emotions using a minimum of words. The book's title comes from the fact that Frieda misunderstood people when they spoke of poetry, thinking, of course, that they were saying 'poultry.' Perhaps I hope that a handful of people (OK, one person maybe) will appreciate my sense of humor in correcting the title as Frieda wrote it, and the subsequent typeset and printed correction on the title page. It could be all of these things and more.

"But as I sit and hold this small volume in my hands, working its sky-blue cover back and forth, and thumb through the colorful pages with splashes of citron, lavender, cream, and pale green on the illustrations, I think this book has come very close to that vision I had in my head when the idea for Book Eight first appeared in my mind's eye. It is a rare and satisfying feeling to achieve the stuff of one's dreams."

—Carol J. Blinn

Mother never told
me food would be
so hard to find.
On tiptoes, I jump
for blueberries.

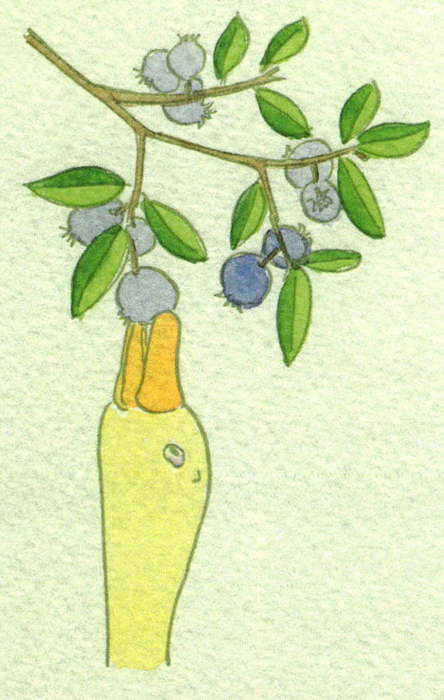

WOODWORKING

TWO DISTINCTIVE furniture traditions influence the styles and techniques in woodworking in New England in the nineteenth and early twentieth centuries: the Shaker furniture produced by the Shaker religious sect that emigrated from England to America in the late 1770s and settled in communities stretching from New England to Kentucky, and Arts and Crafts furniture, which emerged as a part of the sweeping nineteenth-century arts movement in this country and in England, spawned by a rebellion against industrialization and mass production. Both movements emphasized clean lines, functionality, and the beauty inherent in particular woods. The Shakers, who sought simplicity in all facets of life and who centered their communities on principles of self-sufficiency and commonly owned property, believed that "utility is beauty"; accordingly, the furniture they designed and made was well constructed, practical, and beautiful in its economy of expression. It was manufactured and sold commercially in New England and elsewhere in the United States from approximately 1790 to 1840. Furniture reflecting the aesthetic of the Arts and Crafts movement was made between 1895 and 1920 and combined a Shaker-like interest in handcrafted functionality with a love for the warm tones and distinctive grains of various local woods—maple, cherry, chestnut, butternut, honey pine.

While Arts and Crafts styles (such as the popular mission style evident in Stickley furniture) continue to influence furniture designers today, the Shaker legacy is preserved in many of the original communities, now converted to museums and shops devoted to Shaker heritage. In the nearby Berkshires is one of the largest communities: Hancock Shaker Village, with its distinctive circular stone barn, built in 1826. Early admirers such as Nathaniel Hawthorne and Herman Melville came to see the community in the 1850s, just as contemporary artists flock there today.

The Arts and Crafts legacy is reflected in some of the needlework, rugs, baskets, metalwork, and furniture collected in Memorial Hall Museum, one of the exhibition halls in Historic Deerfield, a 330-year-old, carefully preserved village about nine miles north of Amherst. The return to handcraftsmanship first advanced by English art critic John Ruskin and encouraged by English designer, craftsman, and writer William Morris found a New England home here. The Deerfield Society of Arts and Crafts, founded in 1899 (and renamed Deerfield Industries) gradually converted Deerfield from a declining agricultural community to a prosperous artistic mecca. Juried exhibitions in furniture making that promoted simplicity of design, functionality, and the use of beautiful local woods were held annually until 1916.

The armoires, tables, bowls, chests, and cupboards created by Tai Hazard, Walter Goodridge, and Ken Salem honor these two traditions by combining simple, clean lines with beautifully matched and contrasting woods. Hazard and Salem use the mortise-and-tenon method of joinery, where pieces are shaped so as to lock together, held by a wooden peg or dowel, which ensures the integrity and durability of the joint. Goodridge shapes his bowls out of a single piece of wood; if the bowl has a base, it is formed as an integral part of the piece, rather than a glued-on appendage. Each artist adds other influences to these traditions—an interest in Japanese tools, techniques, and proportions, or an interest in reclaiming, restoring, and reusing old and discarded wood. The result is a series of meticulously crafted wood pieces, reflecting both traditional designs and the unique signature of the maker.

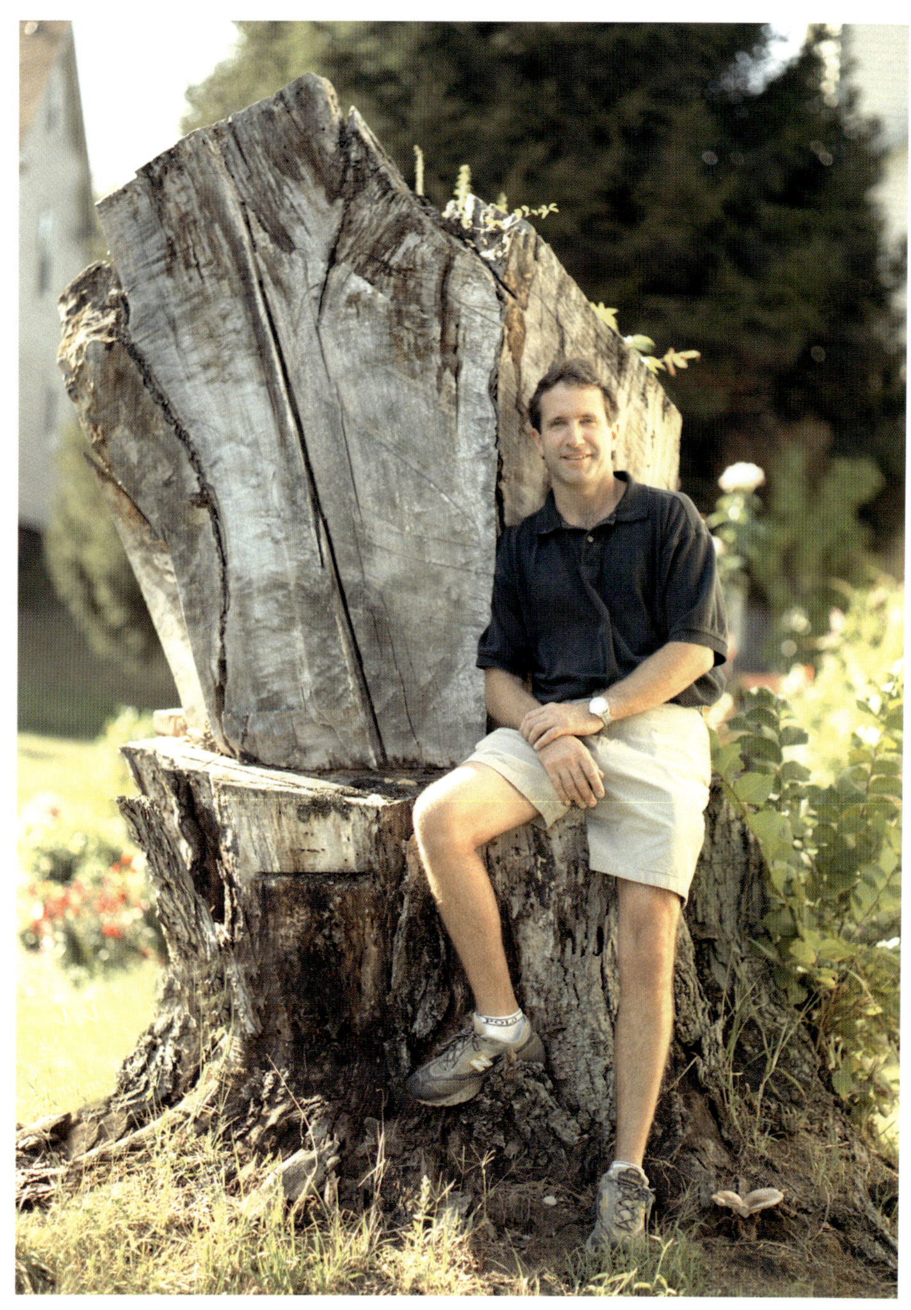

Ken Salem, seated on the stump of a diseased silver maple,
a rich source of spalted wood

KEN SALEM

Furniture Maker (Salvaged Wood)

WHEN KEN SALEM provided directions to his Northampton home and woodworking shop, I didn't realize I'd be pulling up to a stunning structure, one that recently won a preservation award from the Northampton Historical Commission. In 1998 Ken and his wife, Nadine, bought a derelict Bridge Street house, probably a century old, and worked to restore it for the next eight months. In fact, a love of reclaiming and restoring the old has been, quite literally, a part of Ken Salem's birthright.

Ken is tall, well over six feet, with broad shoulders and large hands, curly brown hair and a quick smile. His house has several levels, and the downstairs entrance opens into a den-playroom where Nadine is giving their two children their afternoon snack.

Upstairs, the study features a striking chestnut desk accented by inlays of walnut. The floors in the study are red elm, the walls coral. "It's almost iridescent in the sunlight," he observes. Our conversation takes place at the handmade kitchen table and Ken rubs its surfaces lovingly, almost absentmindedly, while we talk.

For the past five years Ken's furniture company, Salem Board and Beam, has been creating handmade furniture crafted from American chestnut and other "old-growth" hardwoods reclaimed from dilapidated and unused New England barns and sheds. But Ken's love affair with American chestnut goes back much farther than five years. It's a love that stands in sharp contrast to his college degree in economics, the twelve years he spent as a stockbroker in Boston, and the small financial investment practice he retains today.

"Even though I continue to do some work in the world of financial investment, much more of my time and energy is devoted to making furniture," he begins. "I actually find the two worlds complementary, not competitive. When you're totally involved in studying the market, staring at a computer all day, listening to as many people as you want to listen to advising this or that direction, you can make some bad decisions—just as a consequence of total absorption in that world. Going out into the shop, working with my hands, studying the wood, creating something real and tangible allows me clarity, teaches me patience.

"The inspiration for my furniture business is rooted in my childhood. My father and his brothers bought the White family farmhouse in West Brookfield, Massachusetts, almost fifty years ago. My father, in particular, headed the historic restoration of that property, and now the Salem Cross Inn, which dates back to 1705, is on the National Register of Historic Places. I grew up with the Salem Cross Inn and its restoration. I was pulling nails out of old boards when I was the age of my young kids downstairs. I gave tours to the public at the inn and sensed at an early age how hungry most Americans are for a sense of their own heritage.

"By the time I was in college, my father embarked on a series of expansions to the restaurant in the inn; my job was to go out and dismantle some of the decaying barns in the area, available after decades of decline in agriculture. I'd dismantle a barn and then we'd assemble part of it as an expansion to the restaurant. One massive barn I'll never forget: one hundred fifty feet long, fifty feet wide, three stories tall. It was like walking into a Gothic cathedral. It took two summers to take it down and I had four guys working with me.

"That was my first exposure to American chestnut. Do you know it?" I nod a tentative yes. "I'll show you some in the shop. Chestnut planks and beams, so ugly and weathered on the outside, have remarkable wood just one-sixteenth of an inch deeper. Tones range from blond to amber to deep brown, and it's a particularly strong hardwood. That durability and its abundance on the East Coast made it the frequent choice of building material by the settlers. Then in 1904 a blight on the chestnut was discovered, first in New York's Central Park; it spread very rapidly and all but eliminated this gorgeous tree on the eastern seaboard by the 1920s.

"So I had this ingrained respect for wood, even though my college training at Union College was in economics and my vocation appeared to be financial investment work. Then my father fell ill. His battle with cancer brought me back to help out at the inn. I think it's fair to say that his illness was a catalyst for change, but I must also add that I wasn't content in the business world. Financial advising is built on trust; clients frequently become friends. And then something arbitrary happens, some financial trapdoor opens, and that trust is compromised. I found that awfully frustrating, not the way I wanted to live my life. So once I was back into the world of historic restoration, I decided to strike out to create my own destiny: furniture making.

"I mostly taught myself; I read books, experimented, looked at Shaker designs and Arts and Crafts designs—their clean lines and spotlighting of wood really appeal to me. I built a bed that I can show you upstairs, all done by hand. Even though there were lots of imperfections in the joinery, it was a start. And my wife encouraged me in every way. I couldn't have made a shift like this without her.

"Once I began, my experience as a tour guide at the inn came back into my head, how interested people were in some features of the history of the place. For example, I'd show them the vertical paneling on the walls that looked like this." He draws a picture showing one board

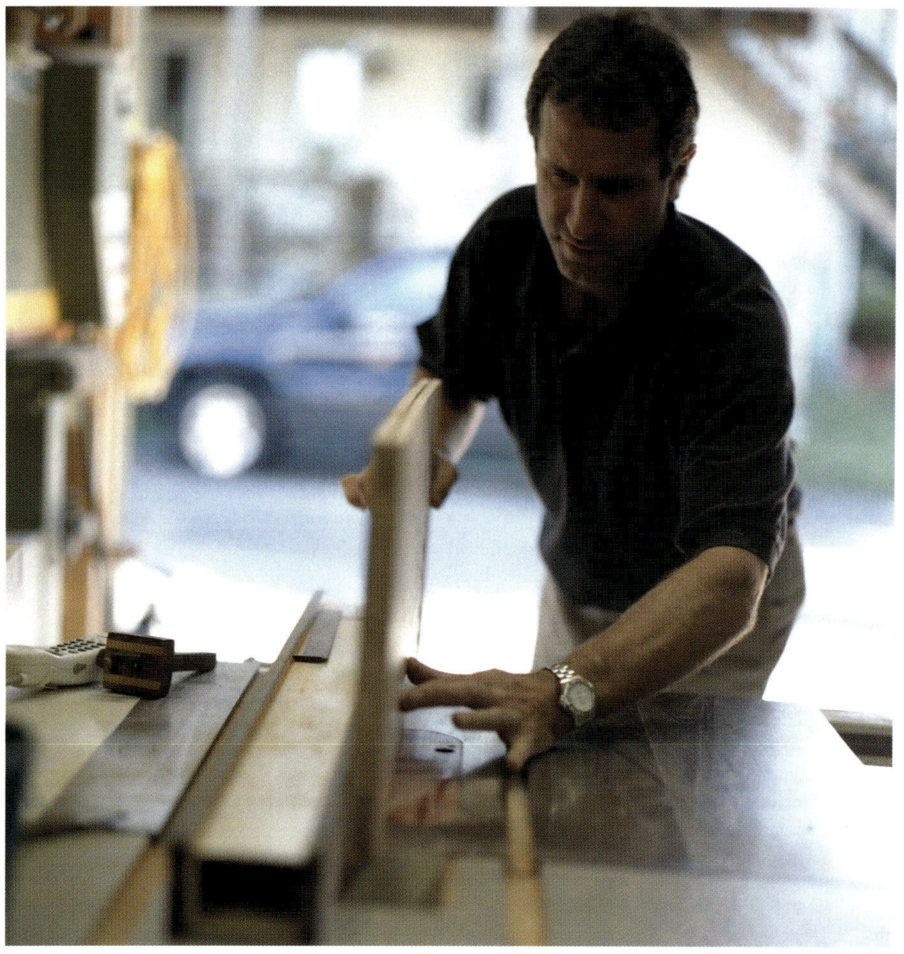

"Chestnut planks, so weathered on the outside, have remarkably beautiful wood just one-sixteenth of an inch underneath."

narrow at the top and fat at the bottom juxtaposed with the next board, fat at the top and narrow at the bottom. "I'd say, 'Why was this done?' I'd get all kinds of guesses. Then I'd give them the explanation. Trees are fat at the bottom and taper as they grow taller. The settlers were frugal, unwilling to saw off even three or four inches of perfectly good timber, so instead of making the boards parallel, they flip-flopped them, leaving them in the shape in which they grew."

He leans forward, speaking enthusiastically.

"Do you know about paintings done by journeying artists? No? Well, many of the paintings we had at the inn were done by journeying artists. Travel, especially in the winter, was very difficult for the colonists. So during the winter months artists would stay at home and execute paintings of dozens of bodies and backgrounds. In the summer when they'd make their rounds and encounter a candidate, maybe a proud parent with enough money to have a portrait of his or her child painted, the artist would select an appropriate body and simply paint on the head."

We both lean back in our chairs, laughing. This is clearly a story he's told many times, one that elicits the same reaction every time.

"People love to know the deeper layer, the hidden life behind the object they are looking at. That's one of the principles that informs my furniture. Each piece I make is accompanied with an historical account of the barn or tree from which the wood was salvaged."

I asked how difficult it is to find these old structures or trees, or even people who know their history.

"With some barns in Massachusetts it's still possible to find townspeople or farmers, most in their nineties, who can remember its uses, what happened there. I scout them out. And I also go to historical associations to piece together the history.

"And sometimes old trees have rich histories—like the huge sugar maple we took down (due to rot) on the West Brookfield Town Common. Imagine what that tree saw during its lifetime. Or the American black walnut tree we salvaged in Holyoke: An Indian burial ground lay across the street from that tree, and on abutting grounds lay the area that changed the way paleontologists thought about dinosaurs. In the

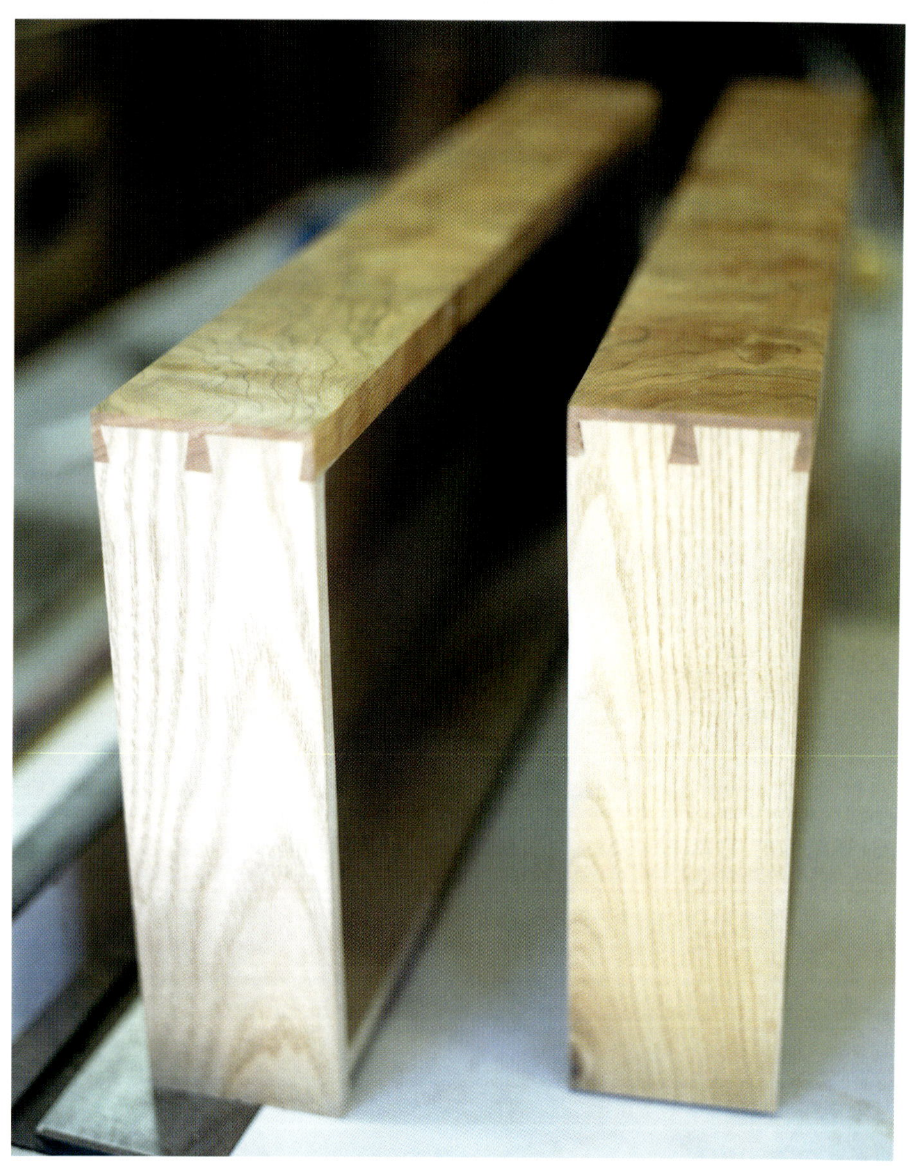

Drawers with dovetailed joinery, one of the signatures of Ken's furniture

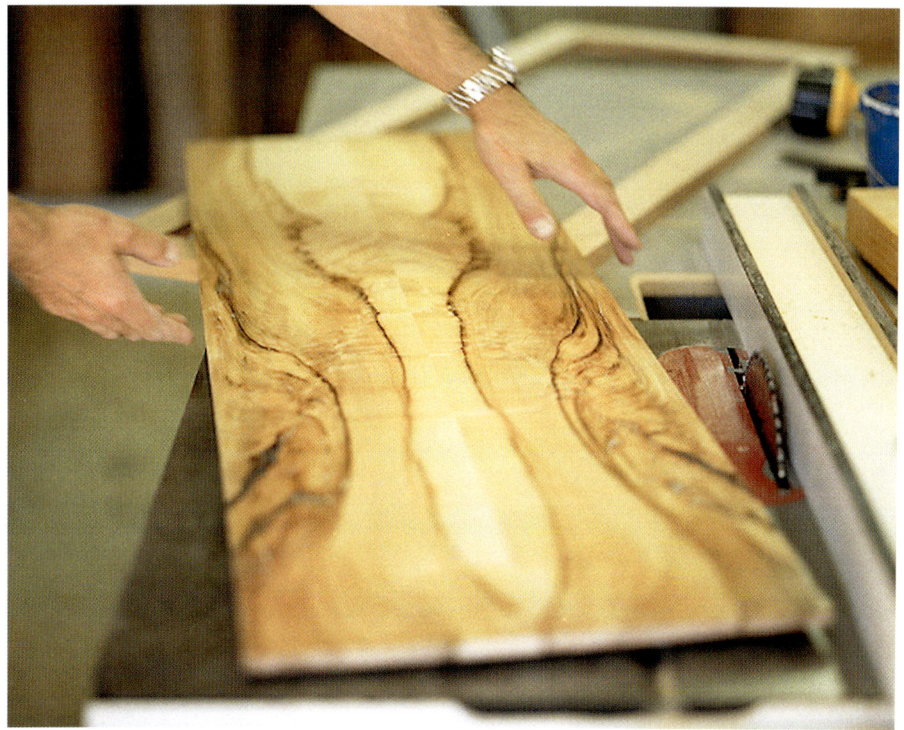

Spalted wood, prized by woodworkers for striking inlays in furniture

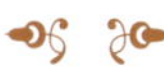

past, dinosaurs were not thought to be gregarious, but the footprints in this area—multiple tracks of multiple coexisting dinosaurs—completely changed that hypothesis."

As we walk out to Ken's shop in the backyard, he points out the decaying stump of a very old silver maple. "There were lots of trees out back here that needed to go when I was renovating the place, but when I inspected the wood of this tree, I was excited to find it 'spalted.'"

Spalted is a condition, he explains, that is caused by fungal disease

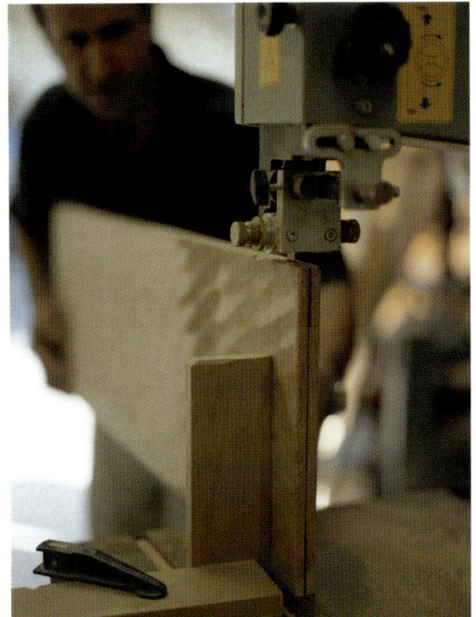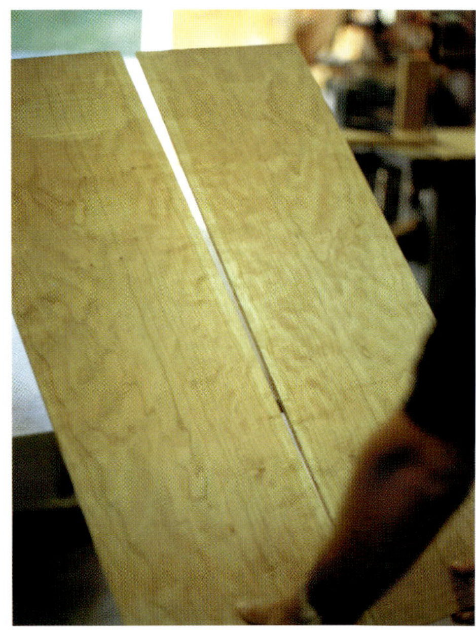

Cutting wood for bookmatching, where a single piece of wood provides two perfectly matched, side-by-side inlays (left). Bookmatching inlays ready for use (right).

that discolors the wood in interesting patterns, bleaching it out in some areas and creating dark zigzagging lines in other areas: It is highly prized as an inlay by woodworkers. Moments later, inside the shop and up the stairs where a dozen or more cabinets, sideboards, and armoires stand in various stages of completion, he points out a chest with inlaid doors in perfectly matching spalted wood. This technique is called "bookmatching" and is achieved by cutting one piece of spalted wood in the middle and opening it up to reveal breathtaking side-by-side decorative patterns. "You never know when you have a treasure right in your own backyard," he says, smiling.

Outside the shop is the huge horizontally cutting WoodMizer that Ken uses to remill the salvaged wood. After the wood has been remilled

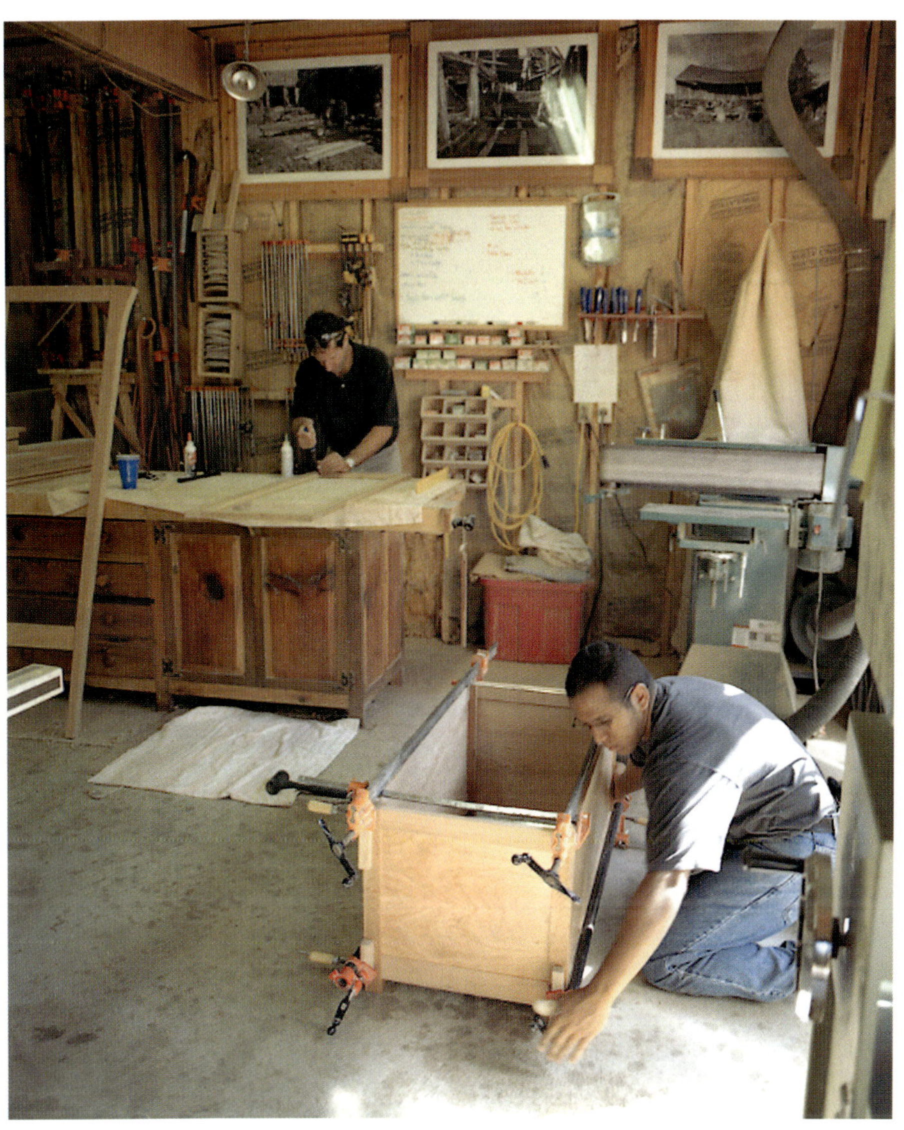

At work in the studio, a converted barn behind the Bridge Street house. Ken and his assistant store finished pieces of furniture in the upstairs of the barn and also on a front sunporch of the house, where the sun burnishes the deep colors of the woods.

and dried in a two-stage process, the time-consuming and labor-intensive process of converting the wood into furniture begins. Ken favors traditional dovetail joints and mortise and tenon joinery. He uses a series of hand planes to finish the surfaces, applying oil rubs to the finished piece to enhance its natural colors and grain. Frequently, he moves finished pieces to an enclosed, sun-filled front porch attached to his house. There the sun can fully bring out the natural tones of the wood.

"I'm opposed to using stains. Old wood emits a warm array of colors and patterns. If I need dark wood, I go to barn planking—the floor planks darkened by years of being walked on by horses and cows. If I want light wood, I go to beaming. I use some other woods like maple, walnut, cherry, but all my sources of wood are 'found,' taken from trees or structures that would otherwise be destroyed. I guess you could say that all of my wood is finding its second life."

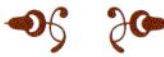

Before leaving, I ask Ken what challenges lie ahead. He laughs and says, "I'm always percolating with new projects. I'll stay in the shop sometimes until 1 or 2 A.M., trying to figure out some problem of design, or how to match woods most successfully. And I'm always looking for the 'ultimate' piece of wood. You never know what you're going to find in an old, abandoned barn. Sometimes when I find a real treasure I just put it aside, study it, thinking up possible uses, a design that will do it justice. That will always be my next challenge. There will always be another 'ultimate' piece of wood."

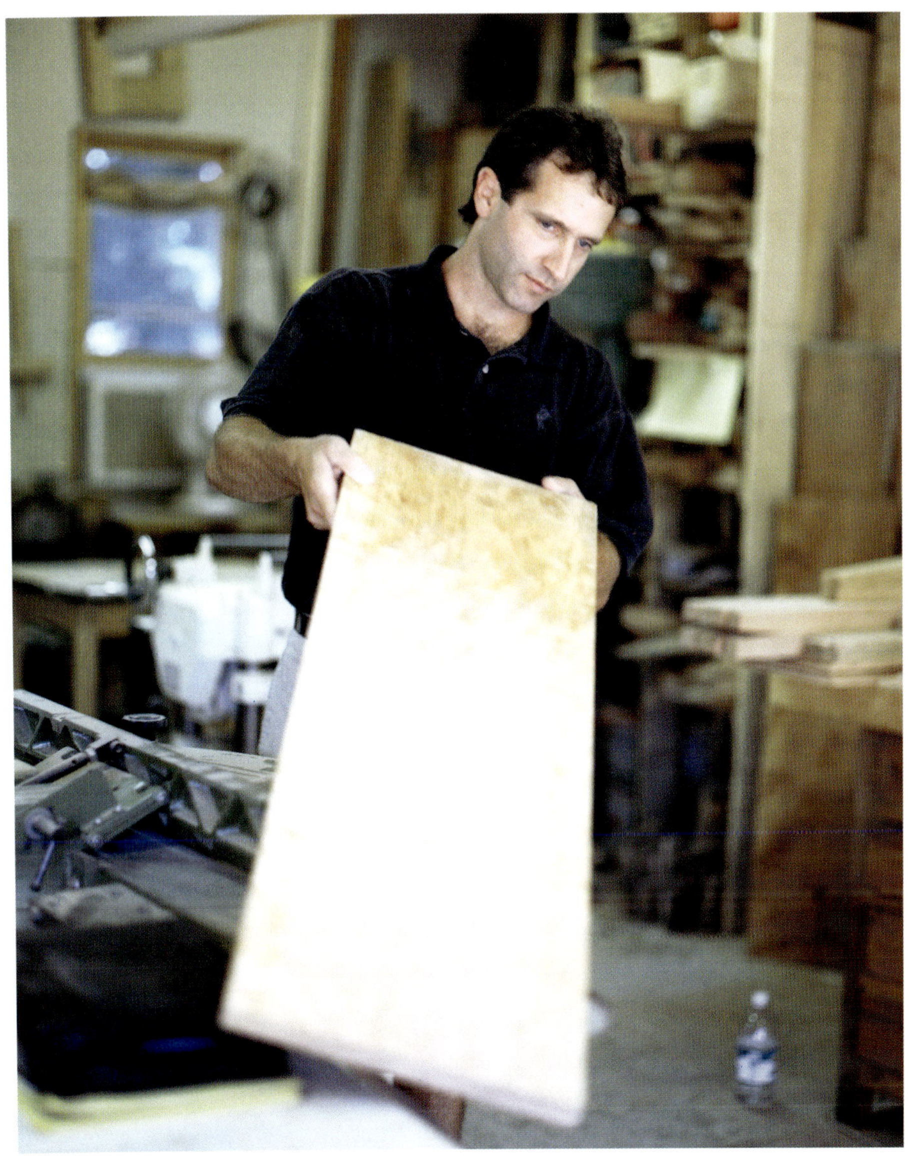

Sighting the wood grains. Carefully matched and complementary patterns in wood grains are part of the aesthetic appeal of handmade furniture.

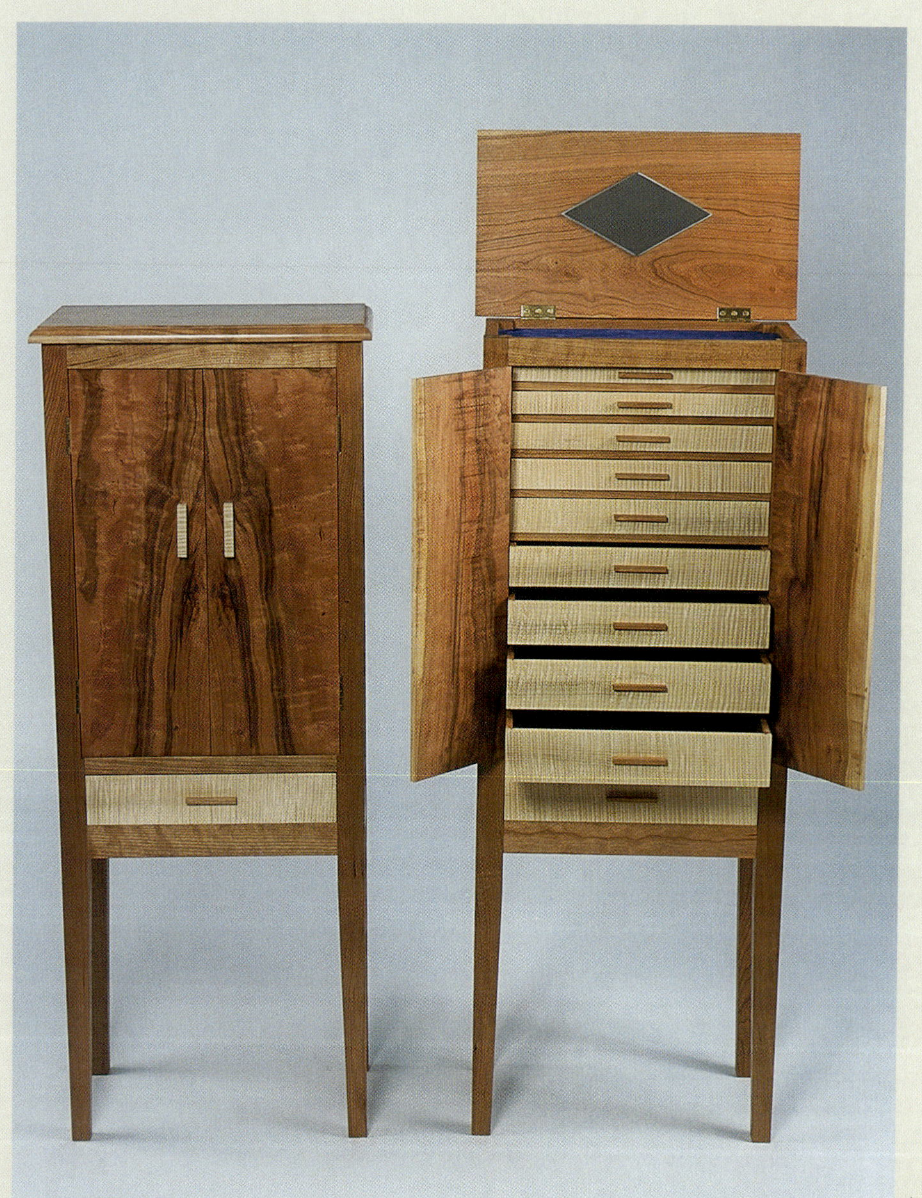

FREESTANDING JEWELRY ARMOIRE

48" × 20" × 12"

"Sometimes one can grow in the knowledge and execution of one's art by meeting the very challenging requests of a customer wanting a one-of-a-kind piece. This freestanding armoire presented opportunities to grow in design ability since it presented a real opportunity to combine beauty with functionality while still satisfying a set of special requests. The customer wanted an armoire to accommodate a large collection of jewelry and she asked for these special features: She wanted the top to lift open to reveal both a mirror and a sunken platform; she wanted all but one of the drawers to be hidden behind a set of doors that would be the focal point of the piece; she asked that the drawers increase in depth; she desired access to one of the drawers without having to open the doors; and she requested that all the drawers be lined with velvet and segmented. Finally, she wanted a piece that showcased the natural beauty of wood, a piece that 'made a statement.' The challenge was to meet all of her requests—which created a wonderful design puzzle to solve—and, in the solving, to create a piece that was elegant and pro-portional."

—Ken Salem

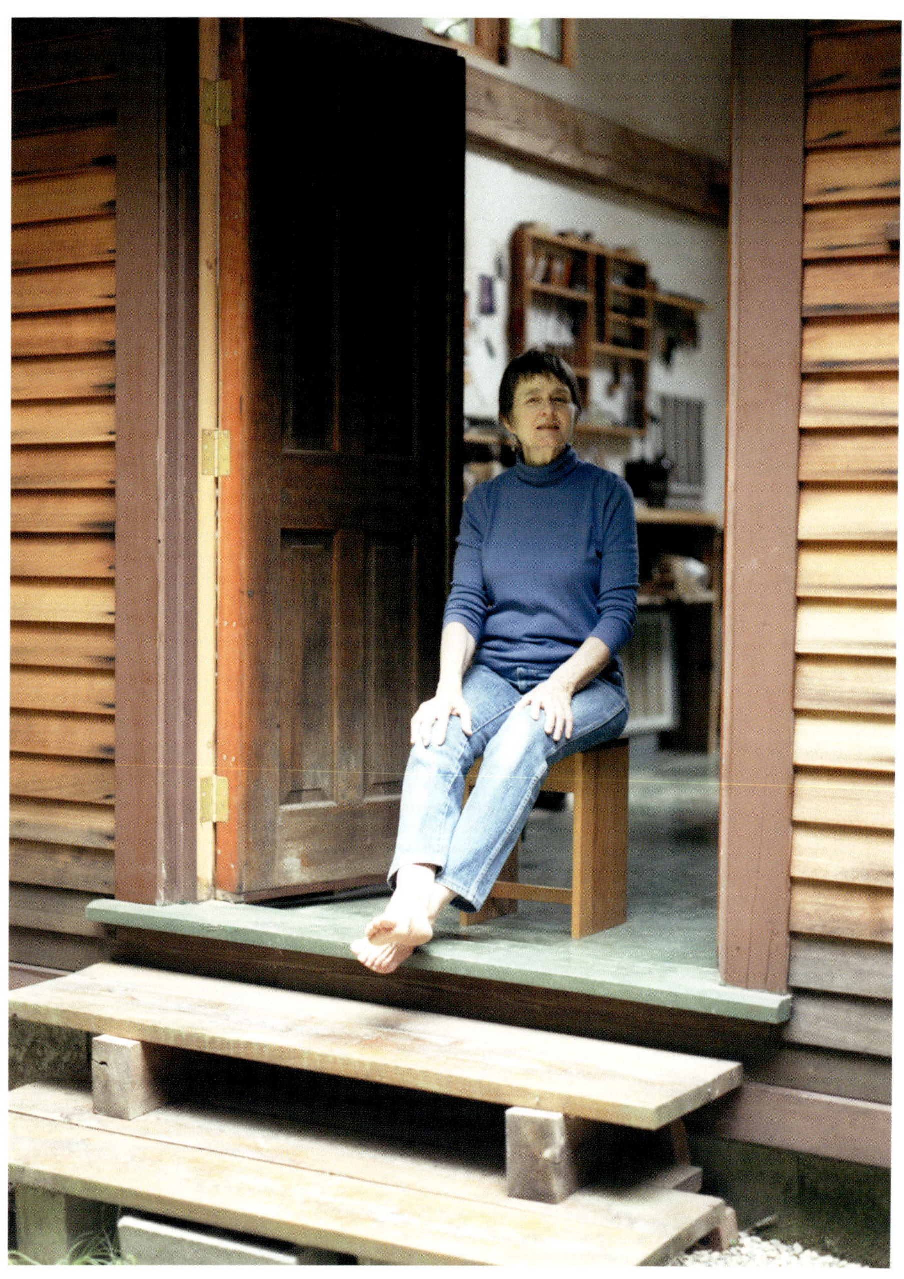

Tai Hazard

TAI HAZARD

Woodworker

As I round the curve in the horseshoe driveway, Tai Hazard calls out to me from the doorway of her woodworking shop. The shop stands about fifty yards from her self-constructed timber-frame house in a wooded section of Ashfield bordering the Swift River. Once inside, I can see a high-ceilinged, spacious work studio laid out in an orderly fashion. Chisels from England, Japan, and a Japanese tool store in San Francisco line one wall; a group of Japanese hand saws hangs to their immediate right. Tai explains that they are called *dozukis* and that they cut on the pull stroke. Their blades can be made thinner than their Western counterparts and the teeth are finely set—a real advantage when cutting fine joints. Hand planes occupy another wall—including several Tai is making herself. We examine a particularly beautiful plane she's just finished, made of reddish padauk, deep cherry, and light maple. When I remark that it is a work of art in the service of other works of art, she smiles a slow smile as if to say, "Isn't every woodworker tempted to make a few hand tools?"

Large electrical saws are bolted to the floor at widely spaced intervals. Plenty of clearance surrounds each workstation. On the far wall, rough-sawn boards stand upended: maple, cherry, black walnut, oak, ash, and the more exotic padauk and purpleheart. Tai buys her wood rough-sawn and kiln-dried, but since kiln-dried wood will try to absorb

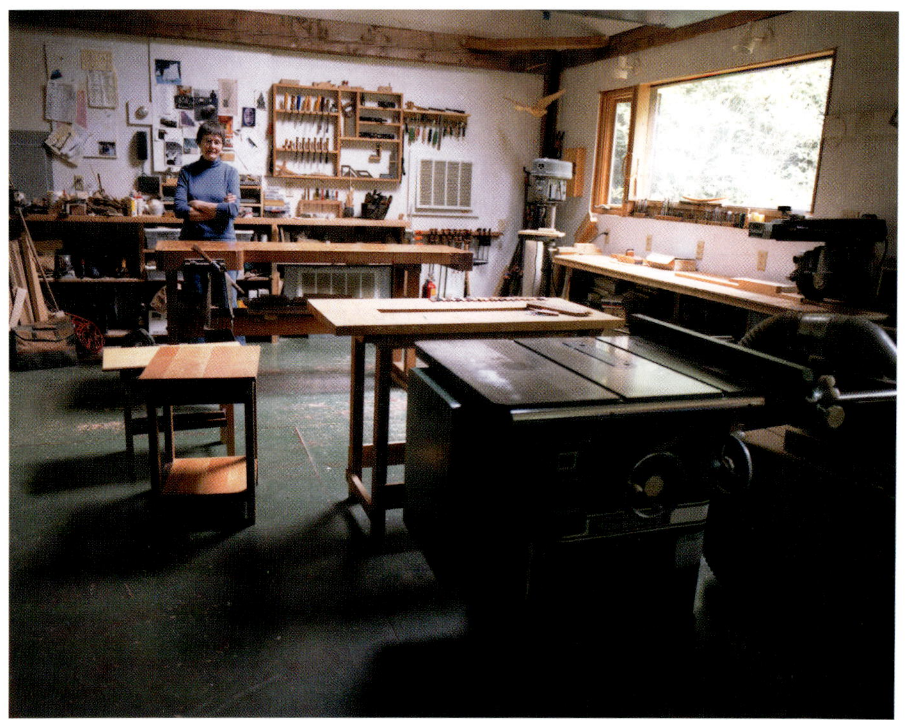

Tai's studio. Japanese saws and chisels hang in rows on the back wall.

atmospheric moisture if left exposed, she must keep it in the environment where it will be fashioned. Clearly, the hub of the shop is a solid but graceful cabinetmaker's bench equipped with a thick hardwood worktop and fitted with vises at both ends.

Back at the house we sit in the "meditation room," a large, quiet room attached to the back of the house, and begin to talk about how a woman who set out in the 1950s to be an aeronautical engineer turned into a builder of houses and maker of furniture. "Craft is in my blood," she begins.

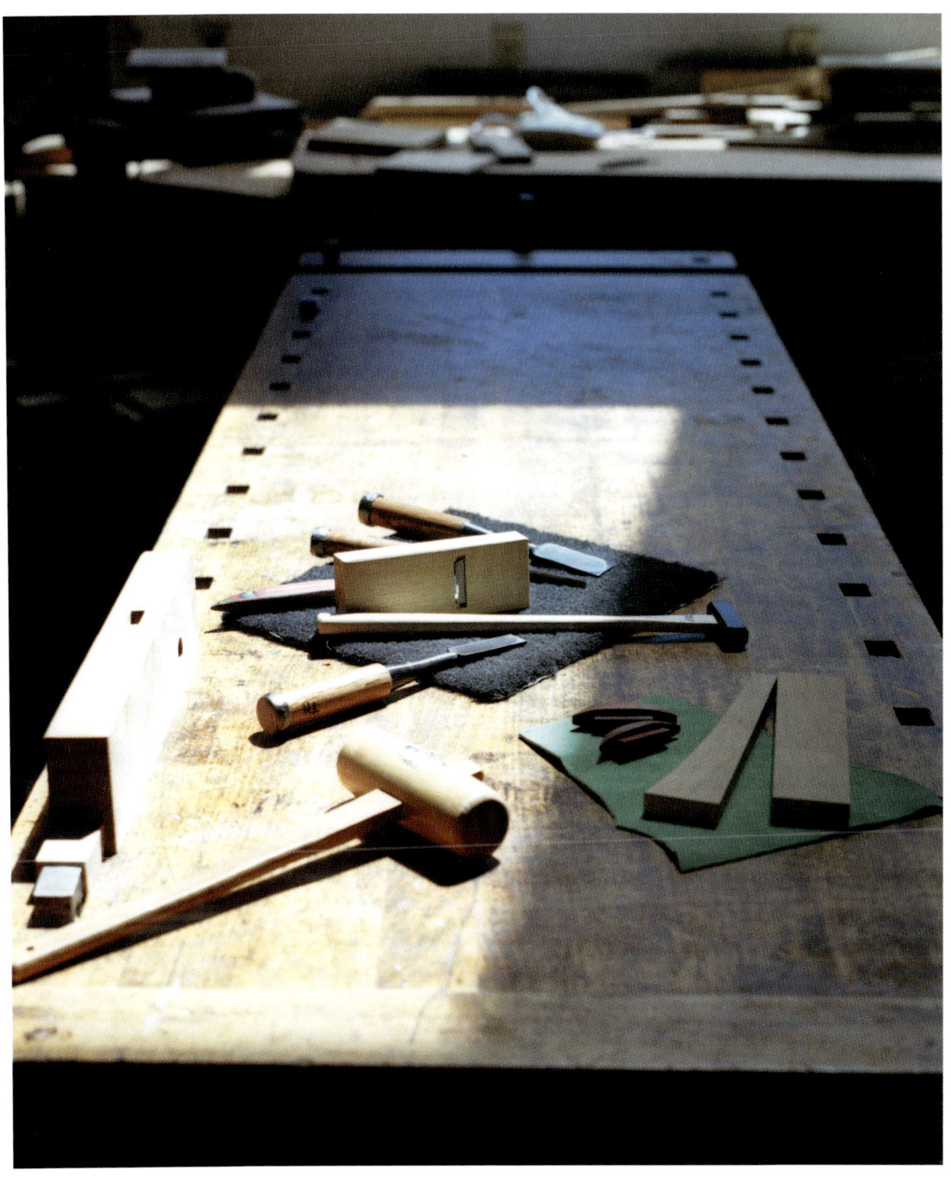

Workbench and tools

Born into a family that valued the making of things, Tai remembers helping her grandmother lay out quilts. Fascinated with the puzzle of matching shapes, colors, and sizes in the pieces of cloth, she found the challenge of transforming them into a beautiful and orderly quilt utterly "magical." Her grandfather and father were "makers" as well, and she learned particularly from her father how to use and respect tools and how to judge the thickness of pieces of wood simply by feeling them. "He made it a game for me, asking me, without using a ruler, to judge the thickness of a piece of wood down to one-sixteenth of an inch." By the age of twelve she could cut dovetail joints and hand-plane a piece of wood to its desired smoothness.

Good at math and three-dimensional logistics, she headed off to Northwestern University, where she planned to major in aeronautical engineering, a choice she observed wryly "was probably not the most appropriate choice for a young woman in 1954." Instead, she got a degree in languages and later a B.F.A. in sculpture. In the early 1970s she completed an M.A. in sculpture at Mount Holyoke, a move that brought her to Western Massachusetts.

I asked how one moves from sculpture (bronze castings, for the most part) to woodworking.

"It happened this way. I was a big runner then, a jogger actually, in and around South Hadley and the Mount Holyoke campus. One day I was jogging down 'faculty lane' when I saw a huge piece of sculpture. It was, in fact, the skeleton of a timber-frame house—one rising three full stories. I talked to the guys who were working on it, saying, 'Hey, I can do carpentry.' They looked at me kind of sideways and told me to show up the next day. When I arrived at 8 A.M., they told me to climb up to the highest point—I went inching my way up these twelve-by-twelve timbers, no ladders, just freehanding it all the way. When I got up there, I looked down—maybe forty feet—and shouted, 'Now what?'

'We want you to cut a mortise,' one replied. 'About thirty feet long and twenty-two feet deep.' There was a very long pause. Then they broke into laughter. I knew I was in.

"Actually, they were great guys. They called themselves the Old Egypt Construction Company. This was the seventies and most of them were former college professors or businessmen. They sang madrigals on the job.

"Later, I formed a crew of women who built houses, but after a time we discovered we didn't have the testosterone to lift really sizable beams. Our houses kept getting smaller and smaller. At the same time I was making some pieces of furniture which generated steady interest among the Mount Holyoke faculty. Soon I was getting lots of orders. So gradually I switched over to furniture making full time. I founded my business in 1978—and at first I was so in love with cherry I used it almost exclusively. When a client would ask for a piece, I would say, 'Yes, I can make this for you and you can have it in cherry, or cherry, or cherry.' Eventually I began to incorporate contrasting woods into my tables, desks, and cabinets—dark walnut, the reddish padauk you saw in the shop. Often that contrast or mix of woods will define a shape or a curve."

I wondered if she, as a woman in a traditionally male occupation, has encountered prejudice.

"Well, certainly in the early seventies a woman working in carpentry, house building, furniture making was pretty uncommon. I'd have to say I encountered some surprise, but not active hostility. Craftspeople respect their craft. If you show your competence, if you respect the wood and the tools, if you're serious about your work, then gender difference just falls away." She sat quietly for a moment, as if she were reviewing the veracity of what she had just said, then nodded a quick affirmative.

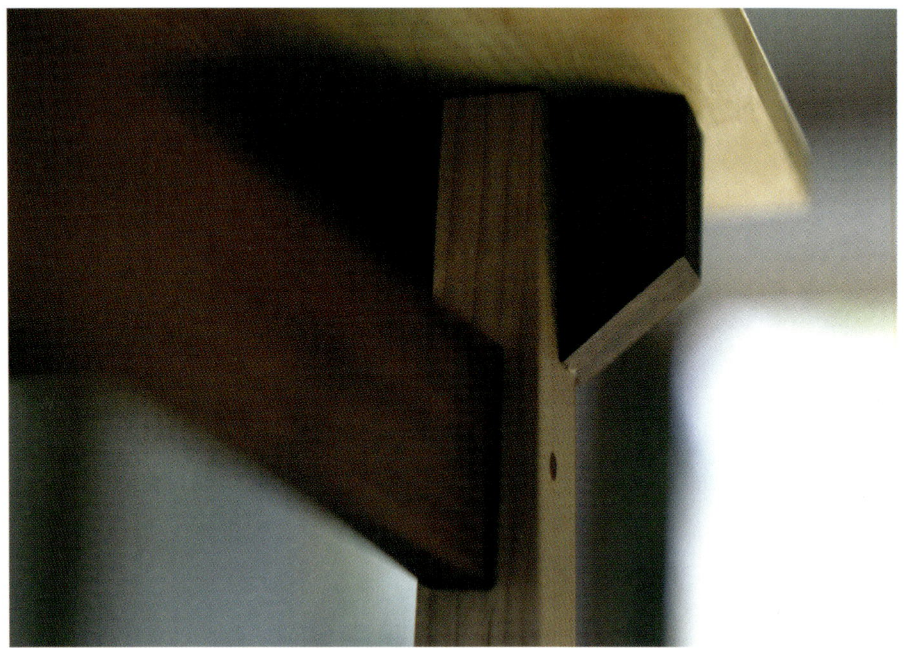

A signature of Tai's furniture: contrasting woods and graceful joinery

Though a member of an artist's cooperative in Boston where she re-
tailed her work for four years, Tai clearly prefers direct contact with
her clients. "I believe that art, my art at least, is communication, not
self-expression. So I want to start a conversation with a client. When
people give me some leeway—when they say I want a table to seat
eight people comfortably; here's the space I have; here's the approxi-
mate amount of money I can afford to spend—then a wonderful dance
between my skills and their needs begins."

She points to an eclectic group of influences on her work; primary
among them is a long and multifaceted love of Japanese culture, landscape, and architecture. She's studied martial arts for years (the spiritual form, rather than the competitive form, she hastens to add), the

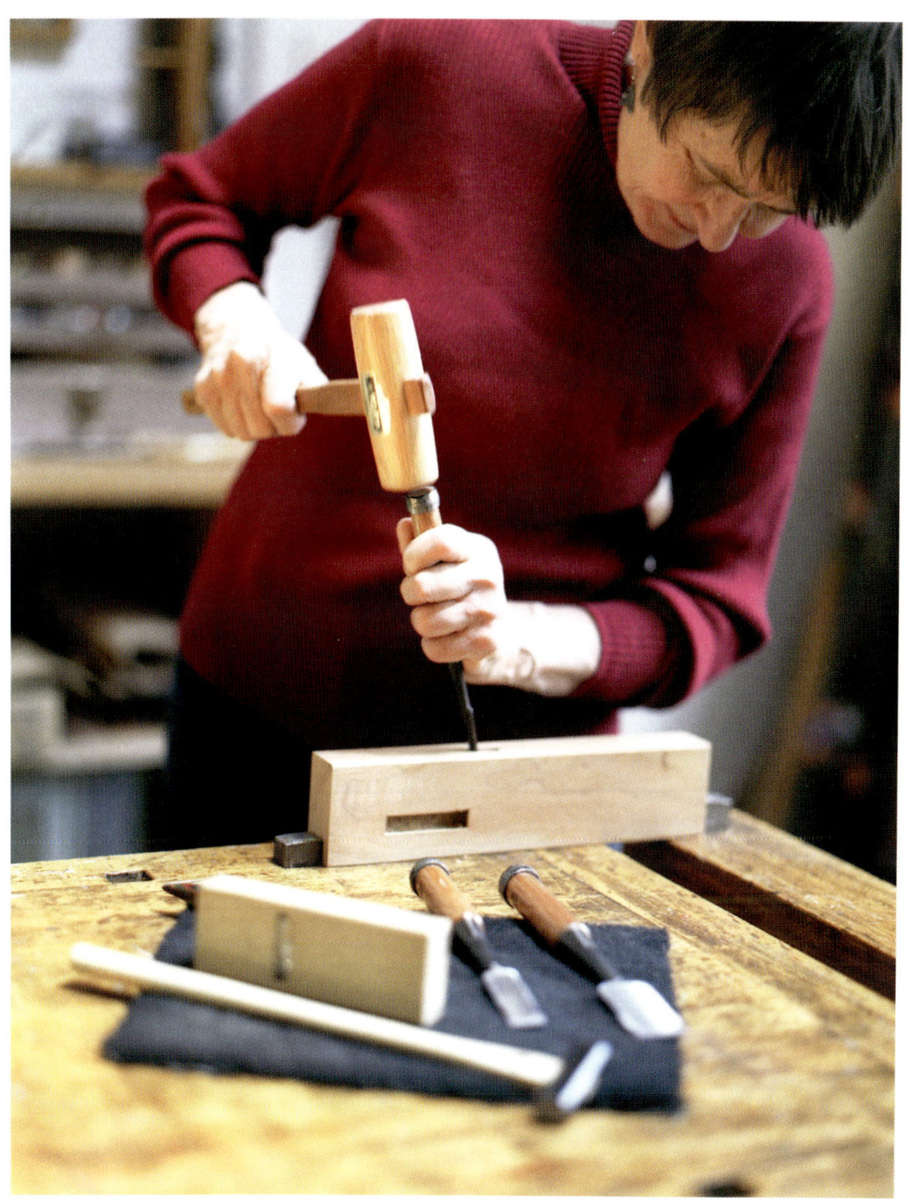

The handmade process: chisel and mallet

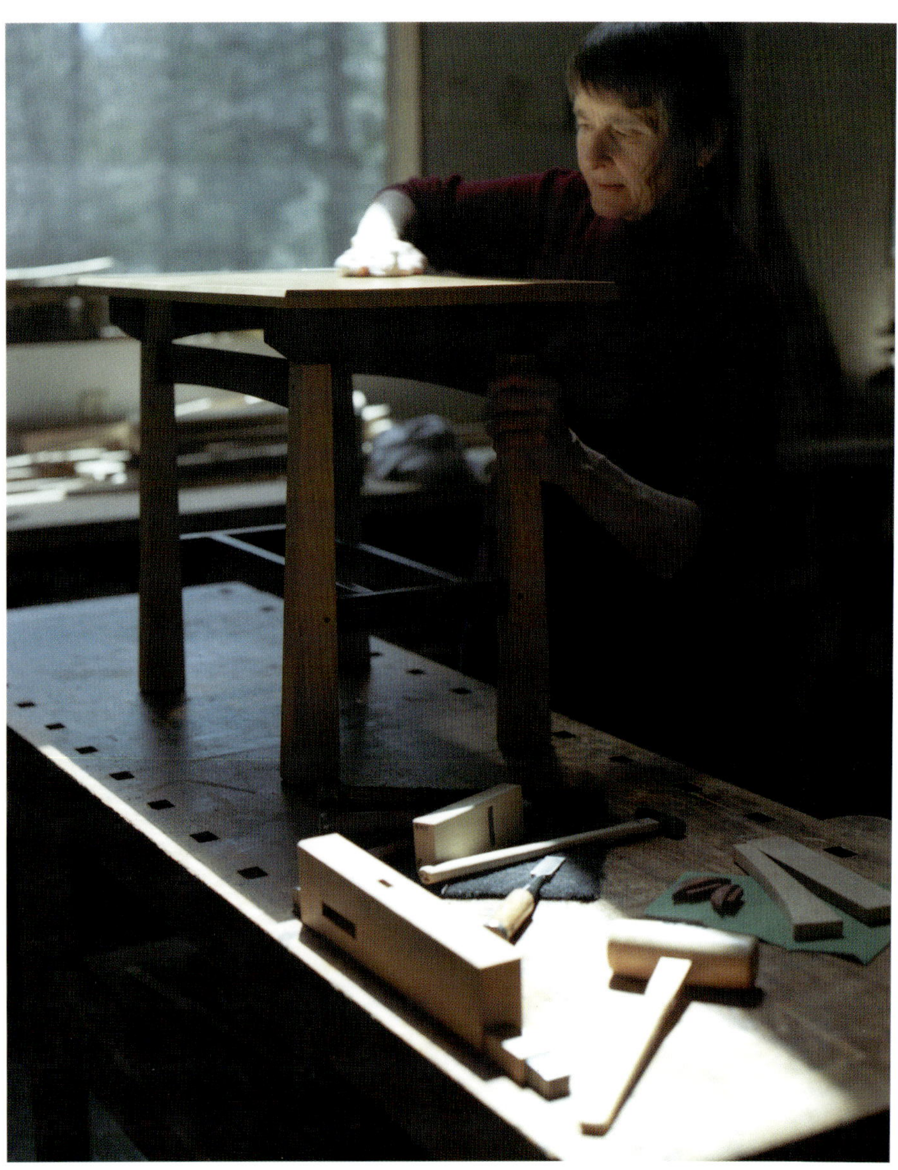

The finish work on a handmade table requires touch. "Match the pieces meticulously, arrange, rearrange, see how they dance together."

Japanese form of archery known as *kyudo*, yoga, and several forms of meditative practice. The physical disciplines of archery and yoga are evident in Tai's fitness. She moves with the balance and suppleness of a dancer. Although she is slim, perhaps five feet seven inches tall, one would never describe her as slight; she inhabits her body with a kind of centeredness, a characteristic as striking as her large, strong hands. She's spent time in Kyoto, studied Zen Buddhism with Maurine Stuart, and was ordained as a Zen priest by Stuart in Cambridge, Massachusetts, later doing retreats at the Dai Bosatsu Monastery in New York State. Japanese culture seems "like home" she says, and the clean lines, proportions, and balance of Japanese architectural forms "touch my heart." Shaker furniture, with its double commitment to aesthetic beauty and functionality, is a kindred source of inspiration for her work.

"When you think about it, life is scattered and art brings a kind of immediate focus. When I practice archery, I know there is a prescribed form, one that doesn't allow for deviation, at least at first. It's all about focus. But when I've perfected my technique, when I can execute that prescribed form—then something opens in my body, opens into an expansive creativity.

"Think of how Yo-Yo Ma plays the Bach Unaccompanied Cello Suites. Practice. Practice. Practice. Then open into individual freedom. Once you've mastered the technique, once you've put in hours and hours practicing dovetails, then you can do variations that are quite creative and that flow from your body as only your body can do them.

"Or think of that Viking ship that's displayed in the Oslo Museum. Have you ever seen it?" I shake my head from side to side. "There are lots of ways to get across the water. You can sit on a log and paddle. You can slap a sail on and move faster. But to build the prow of a ship with that kind of curve, a heartbreaking curve, requires a unique genius, a one-of-a-kind vision.

"I think that's my challenge in furniture making. Seeing something

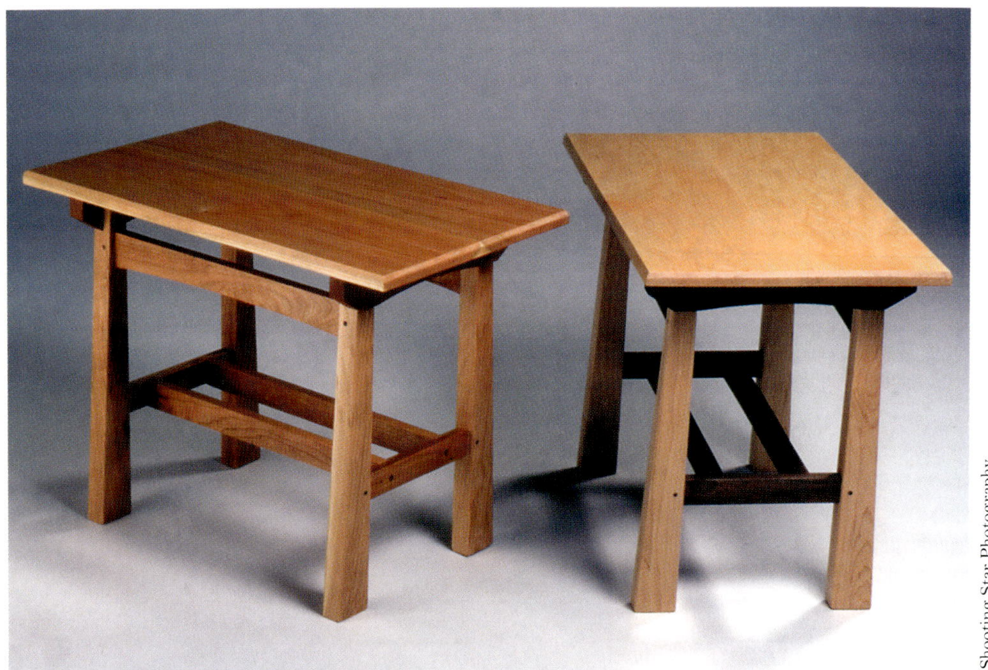

Tables displaying contrasting woods to accent their curves and planes

that needs to be done in a particular way, that is useful, functional, and also aesthetically pleasing to look at and touch—and then pushing it to the unique edge of my creativity. Nothing extra. Nothing missing. Complete."

As I was leaving, I asked Tai what she will do when the physical demands of large pieces of furniture grow too difficult. For a moment a glint appeared in her eyes and she said, "Hitch a ride on an ice floe."

But then she replied slowly, turning each word over, as if she were inspecting it, "I've always loved Japanese tea houses—all parts of them: their architecture, their alcoves, their mats, their proportions. They are built on a human scale, you know, and actually they are getting a little larger—since Japanese people are also getting a little larger. They're measured in units which are calculated around the average height of a person. That's a concept that really interests me: a ceremonial house of the human spirit. Wood, too, has a spirit, I believe. You can treat it as if it's dead, force it through a table saw, glue it and nail it together, or you can take your time, match the pieces meticulously, arrange, rearrange, see how they dance together. I think I'd like to make the formal alcoves, *tokonoma,* for the tea houses and also *tansu,* the little cabinets that hold tea bowls used in the tea ceremonies. Building tokonoma and tansu might be a way of revealing the spirit in the wood."

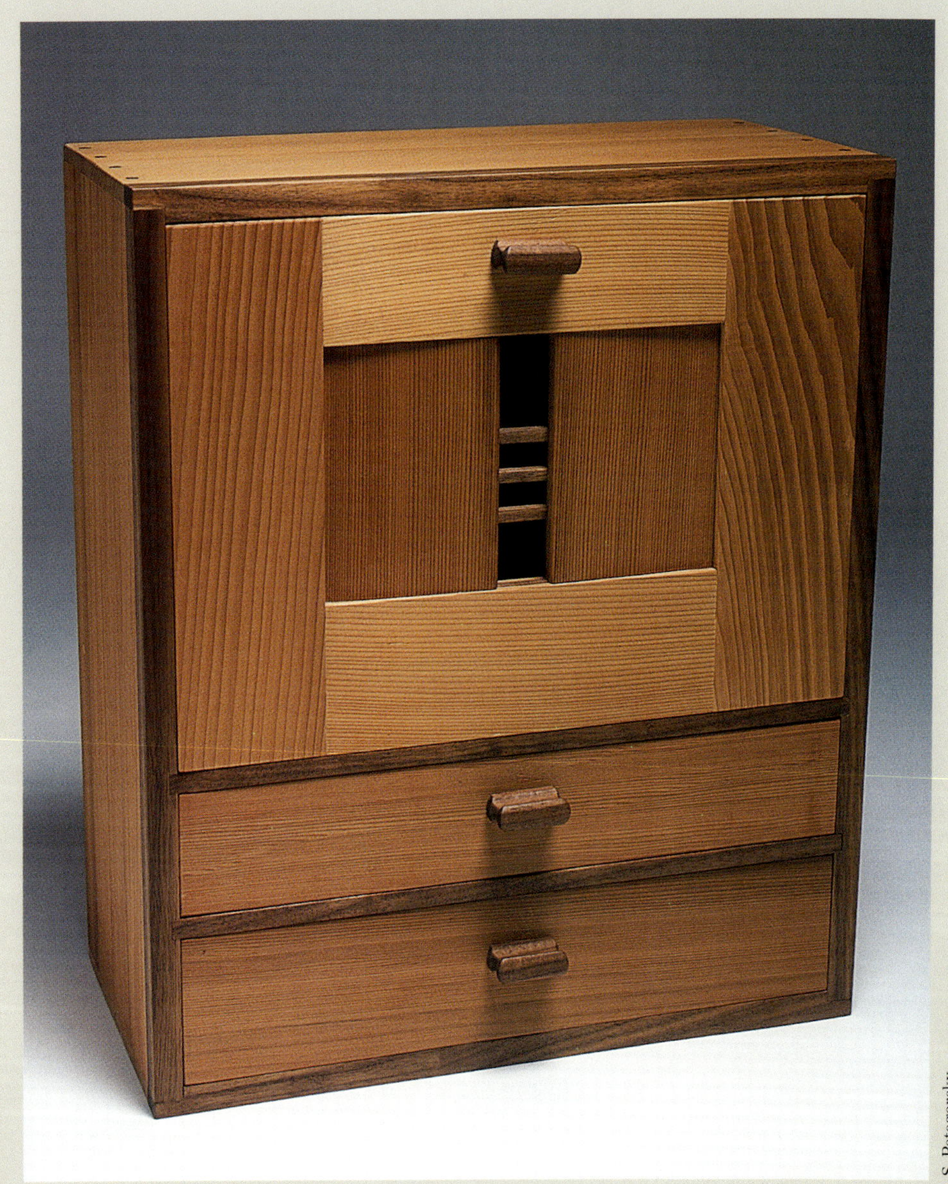

TANSU

16" wide × 8" deep × 18" high,
red cedar and black walnut

"One of my favorite recent pieces is a little cabinet I call a tansu. Although I've not studied cabinet making in Japan, I've been inspired by the many tansu I've seen in Japan and California.

"Tansu is a form of cabinet which originated in Japan in the seventeenth century. They were made to hold many kinds of items: swords, kimonos, food, or sometimes medicines. Often they were designed to stack one upon another, but each unit was relatively small to ensure that it could be moved easily from room to room.

"Building a tansu marked a departure from my larger, heavier pieces, primarily tables and desks made of cherry and maple. In altering the size and weight of the piece, I began to discover a certain intimacy with a cabinet big enough to stand on its own and have a definite presence, but also small enough to pick up and move easily. The softer wood gave a different feel as I smoothed and leveled it with a Japanese plane.

"Tansu can have sliding doors, multiple small drawers, and hidden secret compartments. To me they have a playful quality, one which I would like to balance with elegance. In exploring these possibilities, I sense a certain freshness—the excitement of new design possibilities ahead."

—Tai Hazard

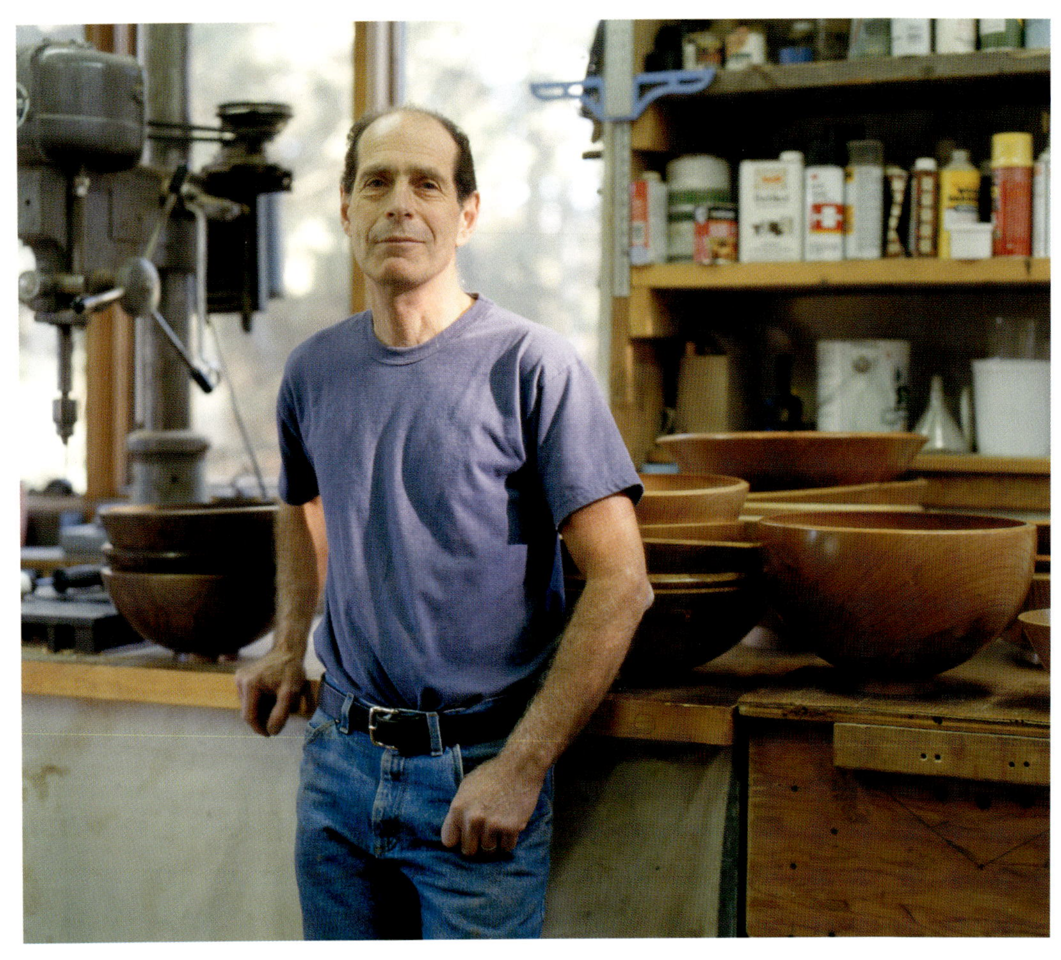

Walter Goodridge

WALTER GOODRIDGE

Maker of Lathe-Turned Bowls

SURPRISE AND TIMELESSNESS lie at the end of Walter Goodridge's driveway. A stony dirt road just southeast of the village of Conway, a driveway not unlike dozens of others that meander off and uphill from Route 116, suddenly opens onto what looks like a Renaissance manor: a large wooden structure topped with double cedar-shake turrets (his wood-turning shop, it turns out) connected by a cloistered wooden walkway to a soaring timber-frame house situated on an upper meadow bordered by acres of woods.

Walter and his one full-time assistant, Bill Haines, are just finishing their work for the day. As they wrap a huge cylindrical piece of wood still mounted on the largest of three lathes—a piece Walter tells me he will "explain later"—I look around the shop. There are powerful machines here and a large microprocessor-controlled kiln, clearly cooking. I walk with caution, only to discover I am being closely watched by Walter's golden retriever and Bill's black and white border collie. The dogs wade through piles of fragrant wood shavings on the floor. The retriever plops down on what must be the best of all possible dog beds.

Their task accomplished, Bill heads for home and Walter comes over to shake my hand. He's a sparely built man, all muscle and sinew, with a handshake my fingers remember for the next several days. He takes me around the shop, one he designed and built himself and clearly a source of pride. As we inspect the lathes, gouges, pulleys, and the kiln, he talks me through the stages of wood turning required in a process that starts with a harvested log and ends with a beautifully shaped and functional wooden bowl.

"I make both functional and decorative lathe-turned bowls, but I like to keep my roots in the functional," he begins. "Decoration is minimal, with emphasis on shape. I want the bowls to be a pleasure to use, so they have thin walls which make them very light in weight. The

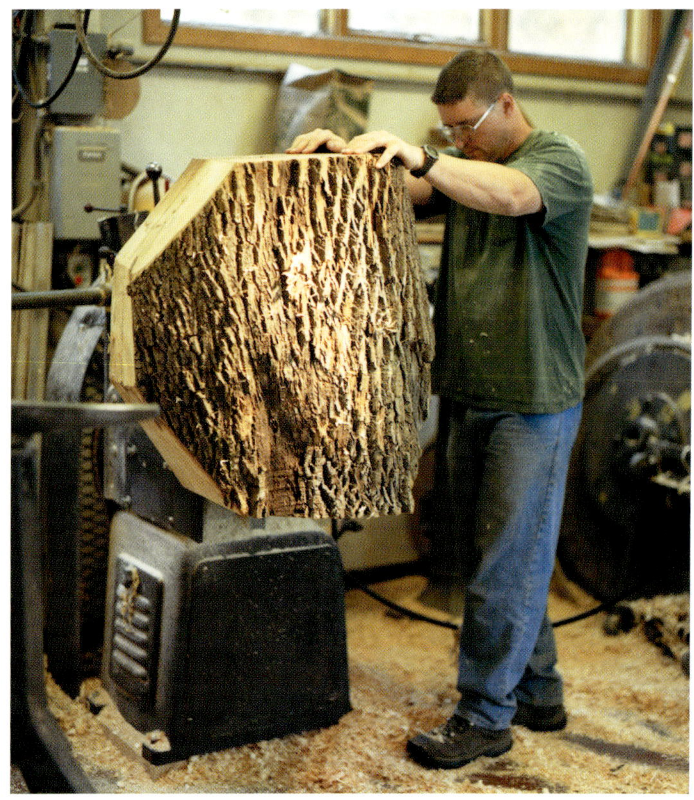

Bill Haines making the first cuts in the roughing-out process

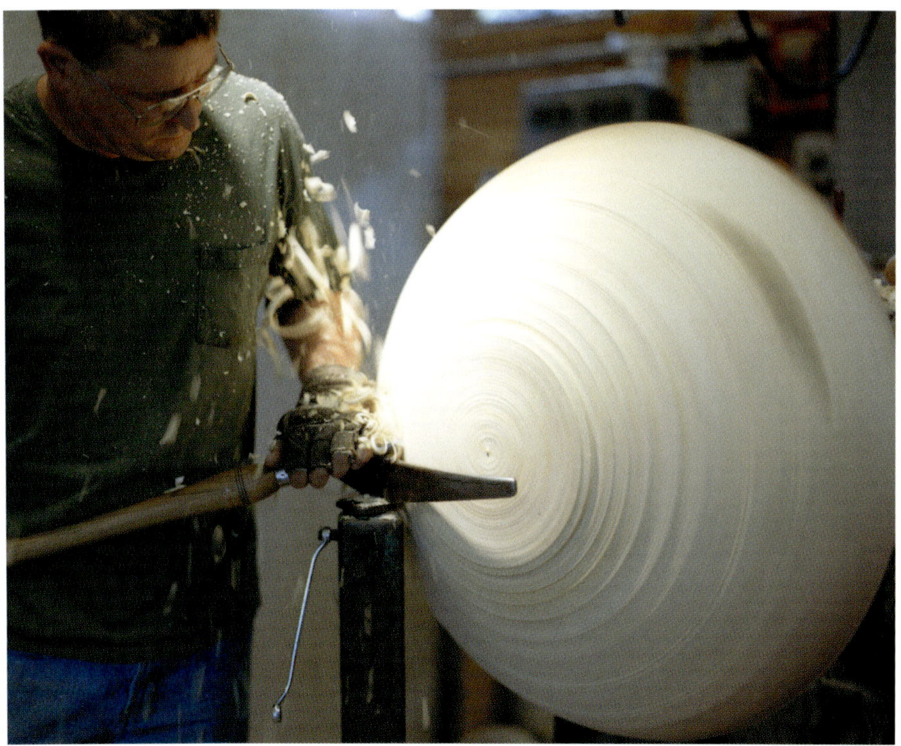

Roughing out the shape of a bowl

thicker rim provides strength and creates a curved undercut on the inside of the bowl, which feels secure when the bowl is held.

"Bill and I are active in all phases of the process. We start with native trees—often ones that are storm damaged or marked for removal—most of which we harvest ourselves. Sometimes the Boyden brothers [he points in the direction of the Boyden Sugar House less than a mile away] have helped us, hitching their team of oxen to skid the logs out.

"Each bowl is rough-turned from one piece of green wood to a thickness of about one inch, its 'core' becoming the next smaller bowl

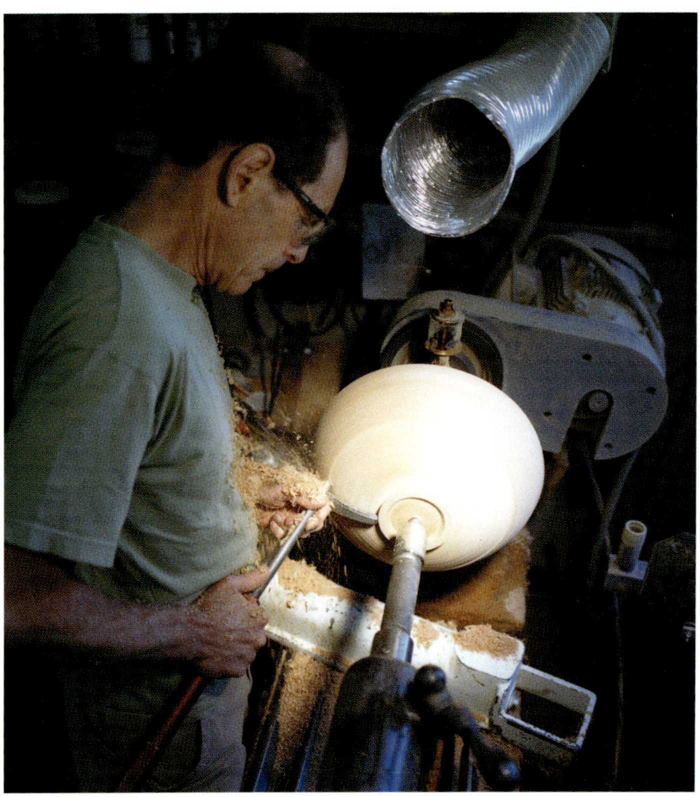

*Walter doing the finish work on the bowl, applying an
abrading tool to the rapidly spinning bowl*

and so on—so that almost nothing is lost. [Not even those fragrant shavings.] The roughed-out bowls are then dried in a kiln which we designed and built. We monitor the controls on the kiln for precise temperatures and humidity in a drying process that takes three to five weeks. This kind of slow, controlled drying relieves the stress in the wood, making it much less likely to crack. "When dried," Walter continues, "each piece is turned again on one of the lathes (the largest weighs sixty-five hundred pounds), its inner core removed by a cutting

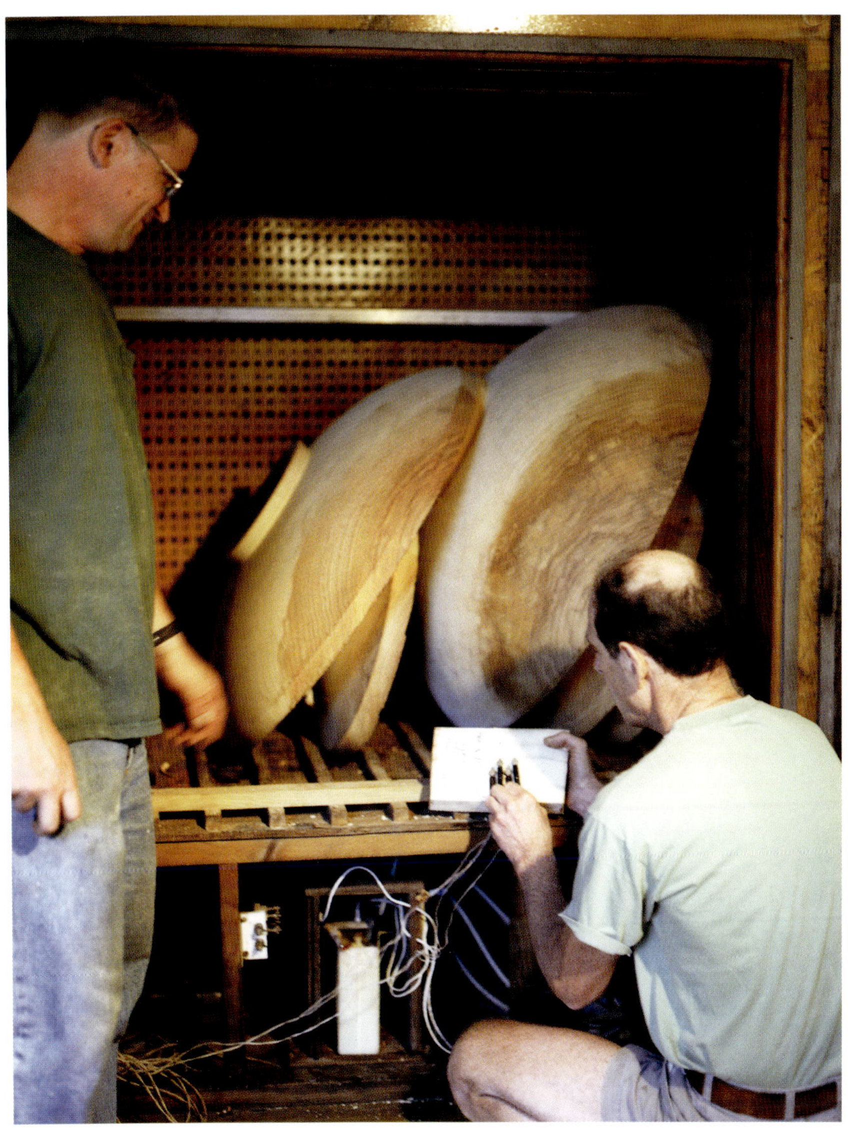

Walter and Bill setting temperatures on the drying kiln they constructed. Heat and humidity are carefully controlled in a drying process that lasts from three to five weeks.

(or actually a planing) tool called a gouge, then carefully sanded and oiled."

I stand for a moment, taking in the whole multistepped process. Then Walter nods and says, "Let's go up to the house for a cup of tea."

A well-seasoned wooden walkway, decorated only with a few hanging metal sculptures and a row of upended cross-country skis, connects the shop to the house. Walter owns eighty acres of land and maintains "miles" of cross-country ski trails on it. The house, with its cathedral ceilings and multiple windows, is cool, even on a humid June late after-

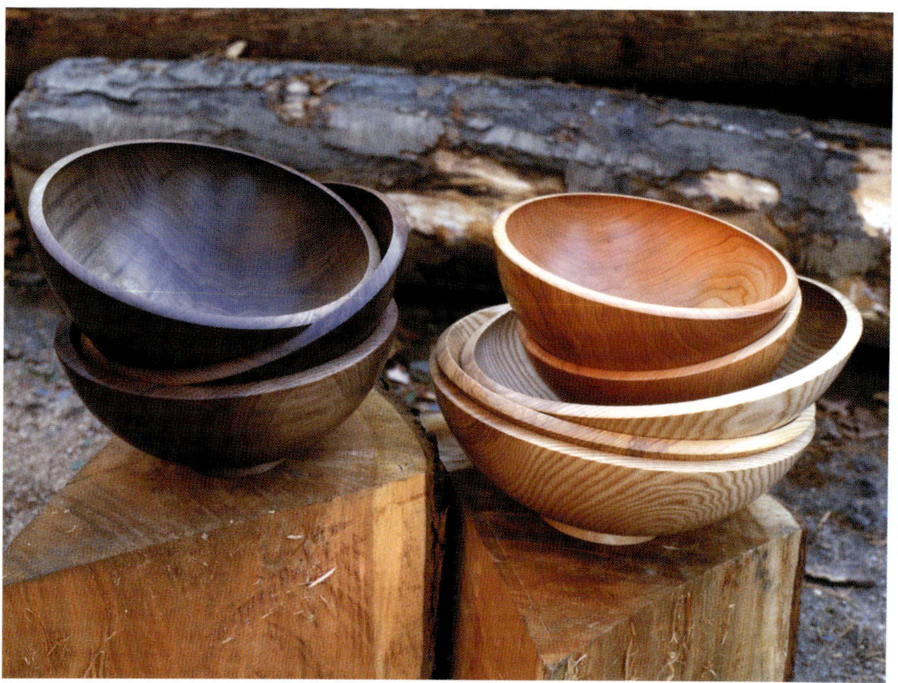

Finished bowls. The bows are carefully hand-sanded and oiled before they are ready to sell or exhibit.

noon. Walter built the structure in the early 1970s, after acquiring the land in 1971. We sit at a long, silky-smooth cherry dining room table —Walter built it, something of a leitmotif in this interview, I am discovering—and are quickly joined by an inquisitive Lab, rangy and black with a gray muzzle and an ever-reappearing rubber ball with a bell embedded in it. I throw the ball as Walter begins his story. He explains how he traveled from a degree in architecture to the work he does now.

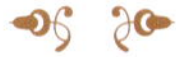

"Actually, it was an undergraduate degree in architecture that I completed at Princeton. I didn't do the graduate work or the apprenticeship necessary for certification. That was 1964 and I was accepted to Stanford for industrial design, but I also had hopes of going into the Peace Corps. You know the turmoil of that time, all the political upheaval, Vietnam always hanging in the background—hard choices for us all. Well, I ended up running a factory in Rhode Island. There I was, just a kid out of college with lots of folks under me, but run it I did. And they sent me to Japan for a year. I think it was that exposure, that whole experience that makes me favor straightforward and graceful forms that have a function—and also a character.

"When I returned I worked for a time in my father's business. Probably his example was formative for me. He was the hardest worker you'd ever meet, a guy who engineered everything. He grew up on the Lower East Side in New York City, was orphaned at thirteen, never went to high school, but through a combination of bravado and hard work forged signatures and got himself admitted to MIT in the middle of the Depression. He took his high school equivalency courses in addition to working and attending classes at MIT and graduated in 1933. I grew up seeing his drive, his constant projects, his string of patents on a whole variety of things, his constant experimentation."

Walter explained how he ended up in New England.

"My grandparents had a home in Dalton. Actually, the property had been in the family since 1772; seven generations had lived there. I spent holidays there, vacations, always Christmas—and even though I grew up in Scarsdale, New York, the real emotional connection was with the Dalton homestead.

"I worked for a time for George Nelson, a well-known New York designer. Initially, he thought he might add a satellite office in Vermont or the Pioneer Valley and I might run it. Later he decided that wasn't feasible, but by then I wanted to look for a place *for me*. In 1971 I spent about three months knocking on doors, talking to farmers, questioning the local postmasters about possible property. Do you know how hard it is to knock on the door of an old-time New England farmer and say, 'Would you like to sell some of your land?'

"Finally I did get a tip on this piece of property, and when I knocked on the door of the owner, I was confronted with almost a caricature of a New England farmer: wiry, miserly, tobacco-chewing, tough on his wife, pocket watch, suspenders—you know, the kind that if you saw him on TV you'd say he was overacting. When I told him my mission, we walked around over the property, I made him an offer, and he— without consulting his wife—just made the deal. I remember walking around this meadow where I thought I would build the house, looking at the proximity of the trees and asking him if he thought I should put up lightning rods. He hitched up his pants, reflected a minute, and said: 'Lightning ain't fussy.' That was it.

"So I built this house and, for a time, other houses in Ashfield and Conway; then I got into designing wood-burning stoves when energy conservation became very important. I later imported stoves from Denmark and was fortunate in this business to be able to save quite a bit of money to help subsidize the new work."

I asked Walter what made him move to turning wood.

"A friend's death, actually. I had a very good friend who was diagnosed with brain cancer, just two weeks after his daughter was born. It was an aggressive cancer which required lots of treatment, trips to Boston, that sort of thing. He appeared to be making some progress—but whoever knows? After about six months of treatment he went off to Maine on a kayaking trip alone. He was found drowned. His wife asked me to make an urn for his ashes. I had only been turning wood for about a year—and not seriously—but this, with all of its attendant emotional turmoil, just drove me. I didn't have a chance to be self-conscious. I made an urn with a stone top on which was inscribed the Chinese character for water. After the emotion settled, I realized that I could do this, that I could travel beyond all the doubts and insecurities."

"It seems to me," I offered, "that your current art combines your love of wood, your manual dexterity, and your skill at designing—that they all come together in a happy confluence. Would that be right?"

"Yes, except you forgot one thing," he replied. "The engineering. The challenge of the kiln, the shop, of doing very thin bowls, or the huge pieces like the Japanese drums—those are engineering challenges."

The Japanese ceremonial drums, I learn, "explain" the huge cylindrical piece of wood I originally encountered in Walter's shop. He's been commissioned to work on three drums that will have diameters between thirty-six and forty inches. The logs weigh about seven hundred pounds when they go on the lathe and end up weighing about a hundred pounds when finished. Some Japanese companies have been making the drums for seventeen generations.

"We're going on seventeen weeks," Walter chuckles. "About two hundred groups of drummers exist in the United States, mostly located in California, although there are groups in Burlington, Boston, and the Izumi Taiko group which works out of the Anshin Cultural and Martial Arts Center in nearby Belchertown. The drums are used at ceremonial festivals."

Walter shows me a picture of a finished drum, a burnished wooden cylinder with taut rawhide stretched over either end, resting on an elevated stand so that the drummer can strike it cleanly, letting its reverberations carry. "It's struck rhythmically," he explains. "You can feel the sound almost as much as you hear it."

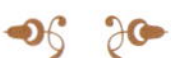

As we walk back to my car, Walter outlines some of his misgivings about his present line of work. He speaks slowly as if to underscore the gravity of his concerns.

"Sometimes I feel in the somewhat uncomfortable position of justifying what I do in a world screaming with problems. Is it right to spend all my days making things that, while they are beautiful, still consume huge amounts of energy: trucks, chain saws, the kiln running night and day. I'm not doing anything for people who don't have health care, or people who have bulldozers outside their homes, or old people who don't know how to access Medicare. Is this a justifiable way of spending my life?"

His eyes hold mine for a long minute. This is clearly a conversation he's had, at least with himself, before. Perhaps it is an inner dialogue born of his experience in the sixties, with its long reach into many forms of social activism. Or perhaps he is giving voice to questions many artists are compelled to address. The fact that we are standing under a Renaissance turret suddenly does not seem strange at all; in fact, it seems exactly right.

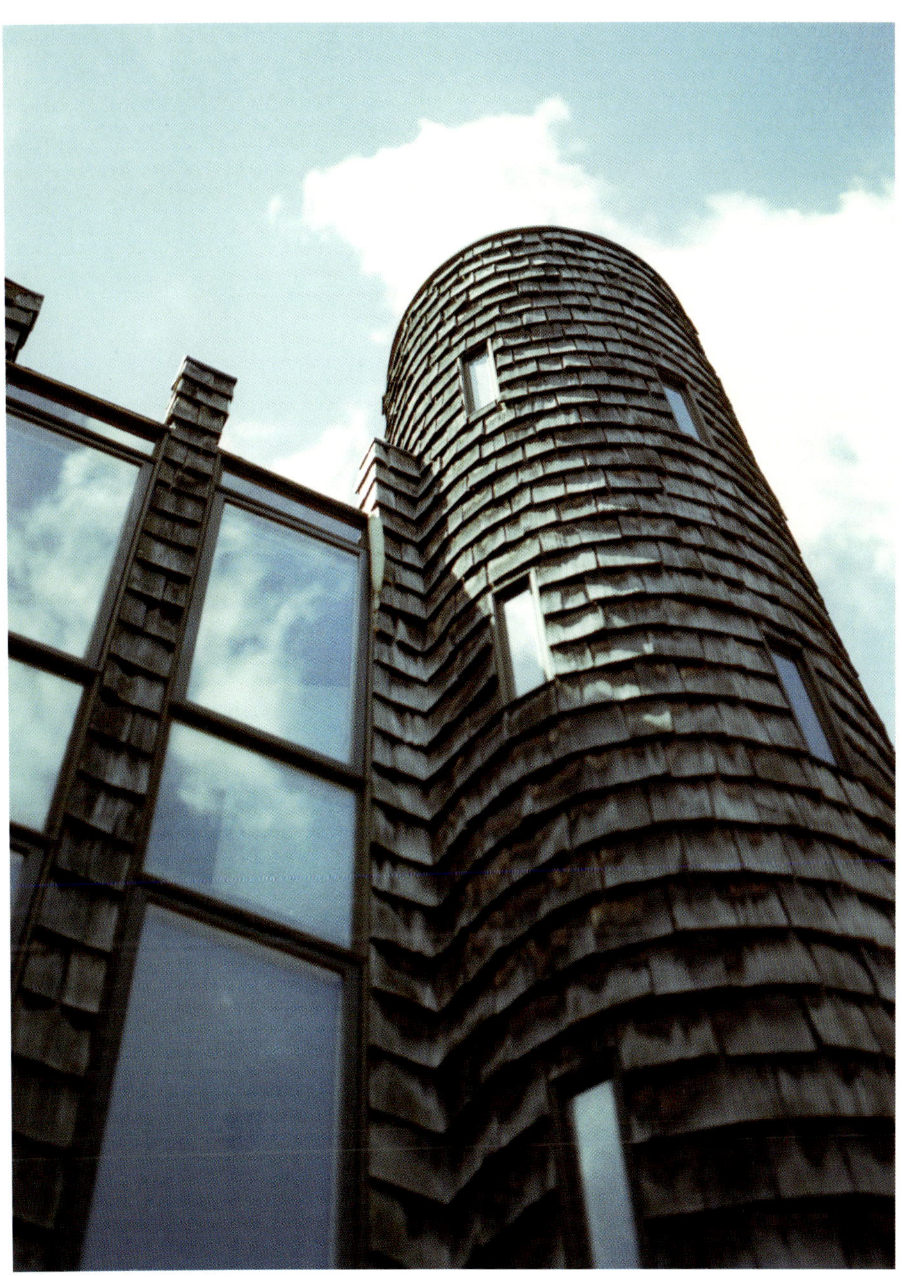

TRANSLUCENT BOWL

13" in diameter, white pine

"Completing thin, fragile bowls on the lathe is a challenging, sometimes dangerous process. A careless movement that would have no effect on a somewhat thicker functional bowl can turn a thin one into flying shrapnel. I started with a piece of pine found by a friend, Jamie Clarke. He knew that highly stressed parts of a white pine tree may contain more resin than usual. We assumed that the resin, or pitch, would add color and translucency to a bowl. Jamie cut me a block from a knee where a branch had made a tight upward bend. Bill Haines roughed out the bowl and the one-inch-thick rough bowl was dried in the kiln at a higher-than-usual temperature in order to harden the pitch.

"That rough bowl sat on a shelf for the better part of a year, waiting for me to feel ready to give it a try. The trick with a translucent bowl is not only to have minimal wall thickness, but also to have consistent thickness. A variation of only a few thousandths of an inch will be visible as a light or dark band.

"The day I made this bowl was a day when, as they say, 'it all came together.' Even the grain pattern cooperated to enhance the flaring, bell shape. However, it was a white-knuckle job, and I actually lay down after three tense hours at the lathe.

"This is a story without a fairy-tale ending. Just after I took this photo, while adjusting a photo floodlight, I fell, breaking a chunk out of the bowl in the process. But people have still enjoyed its beauty and light weight at crafts shows, and since it was not saleable, I still have it with me to remind me of the very special day it was made."

—Walter Goodridge

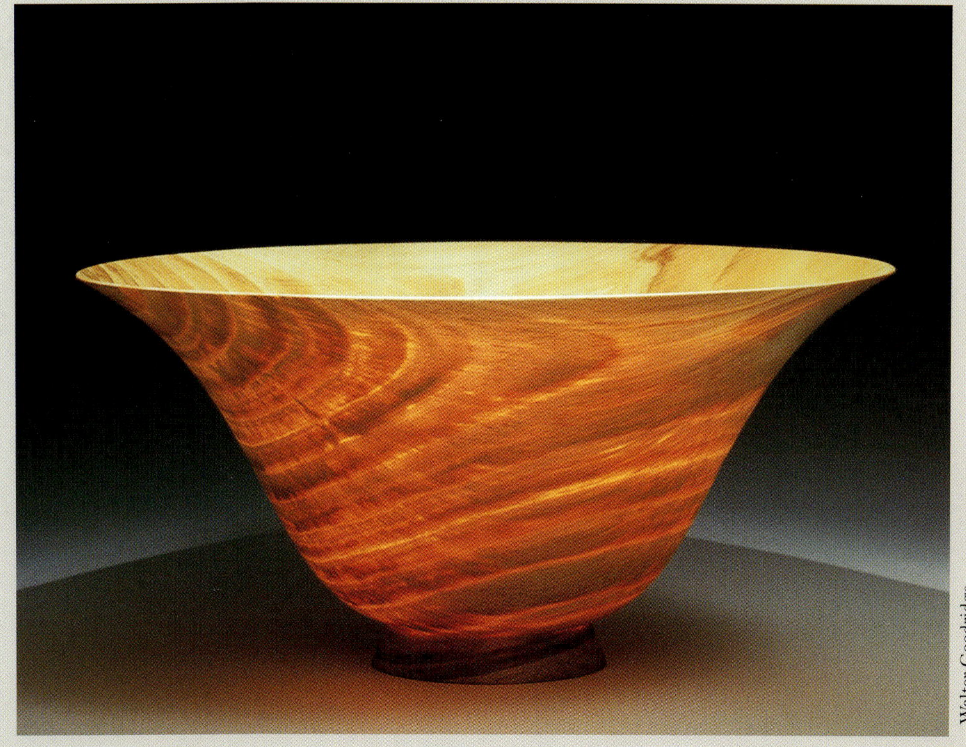

Walter Goodridge

❧ POTTERY and GLASS ☙

AS EVEN THE WEEKEND CERAMICIST knows, all pottery, or earthenware, is made from clay and baked in a kiln; the metal or mineral content, particularly the amount of iron in the clay, creates its basic color. High iron oxide in clay, for example, makes it red, and redware, or objects made from red clay, has been around for thousands and thousands of years. Stoneware, sometimes salt-glazed by throwing common rock salt into the kiln, is a more refined type of earthenware composed of several clays and a glassy ingredient. It is less porous than redware and after being fired in a kiln can become waterproof.

Although regional American ceramics flourished in many potteries from West Virginia to North Carolina to Zanesville, Ohio, the areas around Troy and Albany, New York, and particularly the town of Bennington, Vermont, became major centers for ceramic production in the nineteenth century. All kinds of functional ceramics and tableware were produced at several factories located in Bennington; arguably the best-known pieces were salt-glazed stoneware storage vessels, or "crocks," as they were commonly called. As one who researches and lectures about early American redware and saltware, Mark Shapiro respects many of the values associated with each tradition. His own work demonstrates his belief in the value of making "something useful," and in combining that utility with aesthetically pleasing designs and well-made handles, spouts, and lids. He prefers to fire his own hand-constructed wood-burning kiln when making his pots and tableware. Well aware of his place in a tradition at least as old as history's records of it, he observes, "Clay's low material intrinsic value and fragility, ironically, make it endure as one of the most compelling records of the human touch on the earth. The bottom of the ovoid jug is marked by the potter's two-hundred-year-old fingerprints, just as the earth's strata are uniquely marked in clay fragments by all the peoples who struggled here to endure. I am glad just to leave a record of my own touch in this most receptive, fragile, and enduring material."

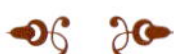

The art of free-blown glass is also an old and honorable one, involving an intricate set of skills. The process involves picking up a glob of hot glass on one end of a long pipe, blowing and working it into a basic shape, then transferring it, while still soft, onto a pontil rod for further crafting. Glassblowing and the making of pressed glass in the United States became a particularly prominent industry in the nineteenth century. In addition to the famous Steuben Glass Works—founded in Corning, New York, in 1903 by Englishman Frederick Corder and Irishman Thomas Hawkes—the Boston and Sandwich Glass Company, founded in 1825 and in business until 1888, attained international fame for its affordable glass objects like candlesticks, compotes, plates, and doorknobs. Indeed, the objects made at the factory at Sandwich, Massachusetts, grew so popular that by the 1920s all pressed glass came to be known as "Sandwich glass." Josh Simpson recalls making trips to the Corning Glass Musuem when he was still an undergraduate, attentively examining the objects on display, trying to figure out the techniques and processes by which they were made. Now his work appears in the permanent collection of that museum. In 2004, he was scheduled to mount a special retrospective exhibition of his work at the Sandwich Glass Museum, the museum honoring the history of Sandwich and its evolution into one of the great glassmaking centers in the country. While his glass vessels, platters, and sculptures draw their inspiration from some of the work he examined in his apprentice years, Simpson's work also catches fire in swirling blue, black, and green patterns derived from his love of aerial and space photography and his lifelong fascination with space explorations. Perhaps more than most, Josh Simpson's work has a foot in the past and a foot far into the future.

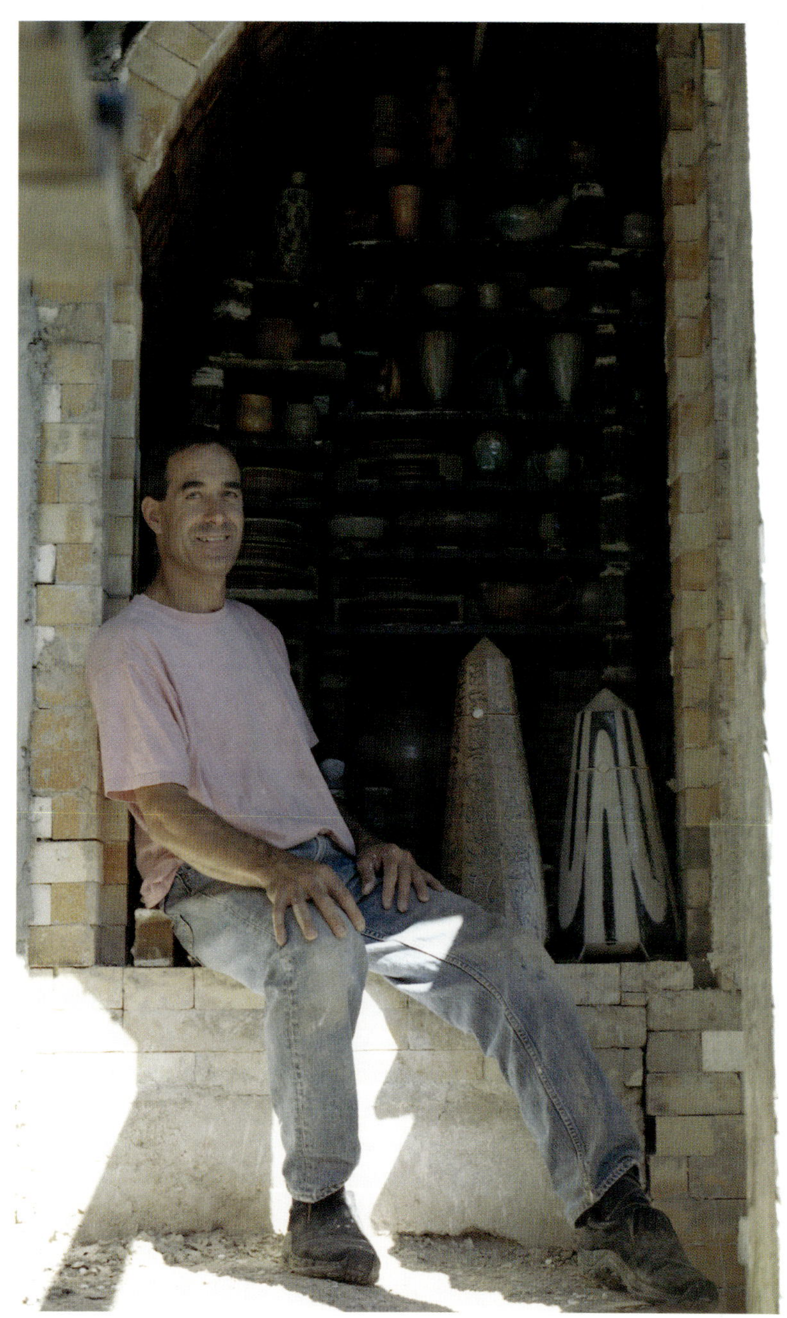

Mark Shapiro

MARK SHAPIRO

Potter

If anybody needs proof that the work ethic is alive and well in America, visit Mark Shapiro's Stonepool Pottery in South Worthington, Massachusetts. In his self-constructed studio, Mark and his apprentice, and occasionally other potters and helpers, work steadily, day after day, week after week, turning out beautiful wood-fired teapots, jugs, bowls, plates—a striking line of functional tableware—and increasingly, for Mark, a set of "presentation pieces," many of which have earned their way in private and public collections, including the Renwick Gallery of the Smithsonian Institution and the International Museum of Ceramic Art in Alfred, New York.

The day of our interview, a humid August afternoon, found Mark at his wheel. When I arrived at Stonepool, a beautifully restored old farmhouse and a cluster of smaller buildings that house the studio, the kilns, and a gallery where pots are exhibited and sold, I was directed to the studio by Mark's six-year-old daughter. Mark met me at the door. Dark-haired and lithe, with corded muscles in his arms and upper body, Mark moves and speaks with a quiet, but insistent, authority. He's a man who has researched his craft, perfected his techniques, and knows what he does and why from the inside out. After setting me up on an adjacent stool, he went back to work on a large, gracefully curved pot, working deftly on its mouth, stopping occasionally to measure its

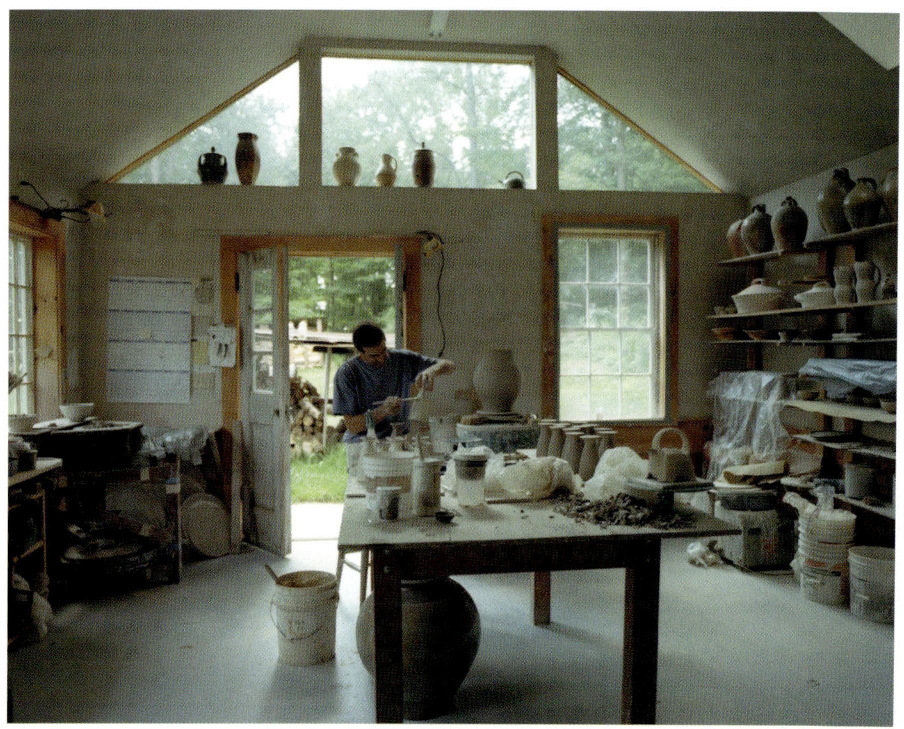

Mark in his self-constructed studio

diameter. Our conversation began as he, and later his apprentice, Michael, worked—because if one "is paid by the mug," as he put it laughingly, and if the work is priced affordably, then constant production is a financial necessity. I suspect work is also in his blood.

When the pot was finished and measured to his satisfaction, he placed it on a drying shelf with several other pieces and walked with me into an open-sided kiln shed, the home of the brick kilns. The double-chambered kiln, which looks like two large igloo-shaped structures joined together, is wood-fired. A smaller kiln is fired by gas. The firings, which occur in April, September, and November, are the focal points in

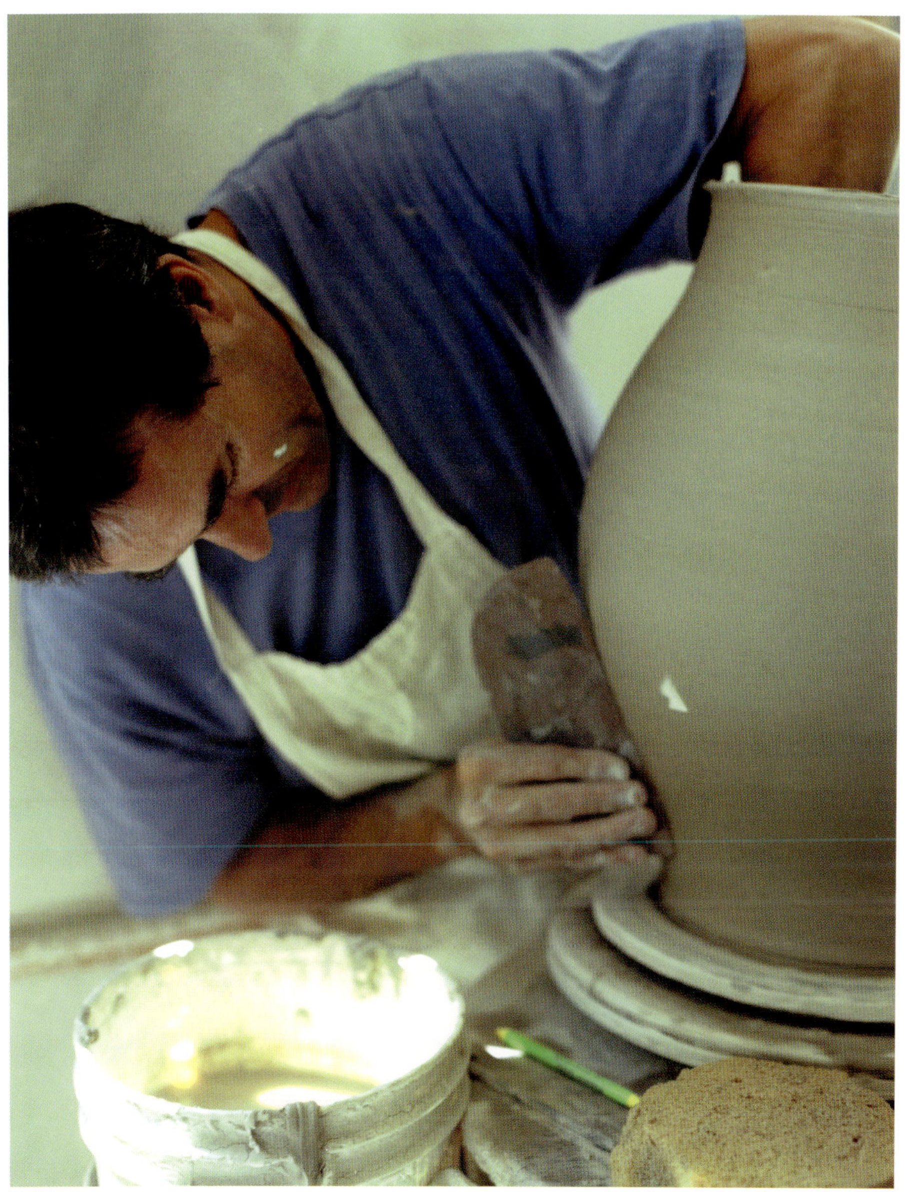

Working on a jar at the wheel. "Clay is the ultimate shape shifter."

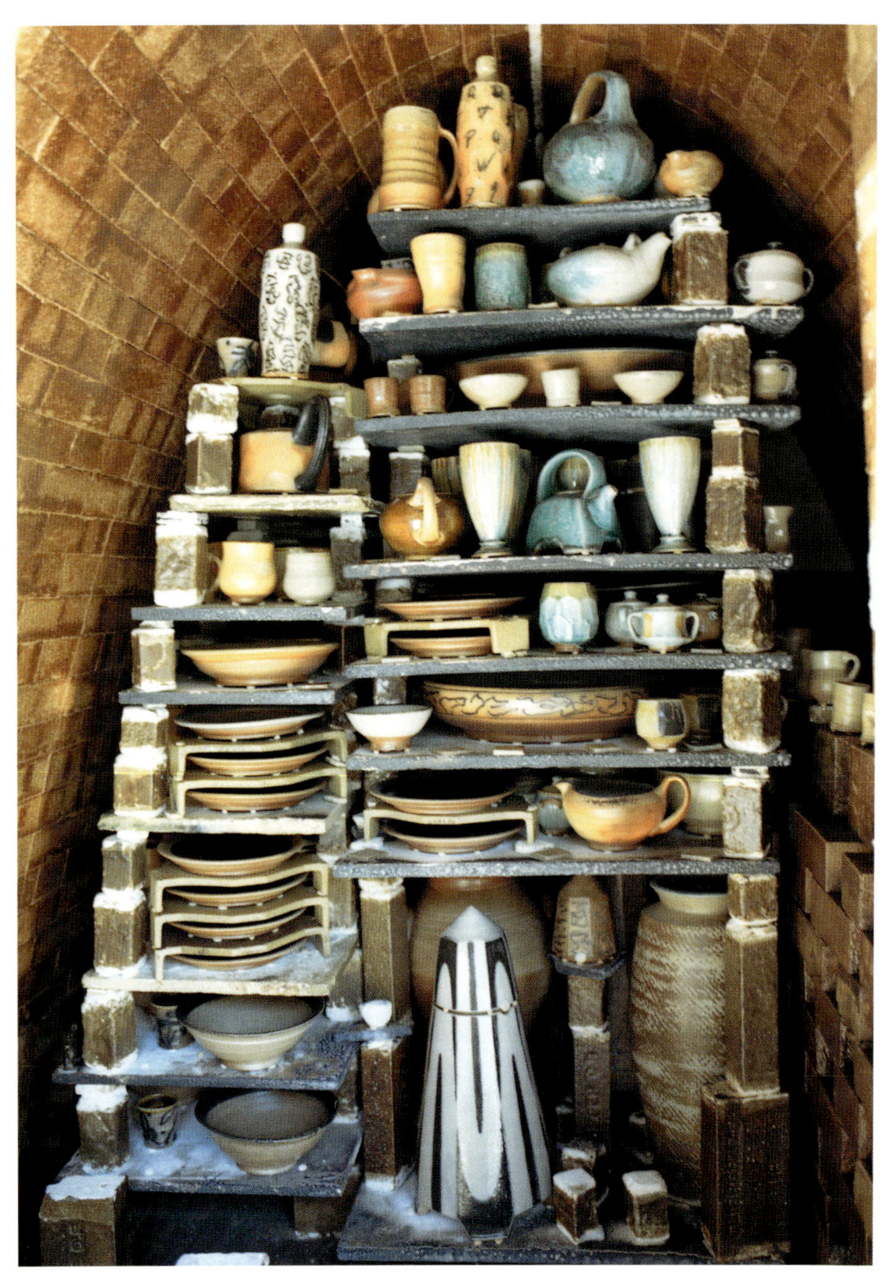

The kiln, built by Mark, partly unloaded after a firing

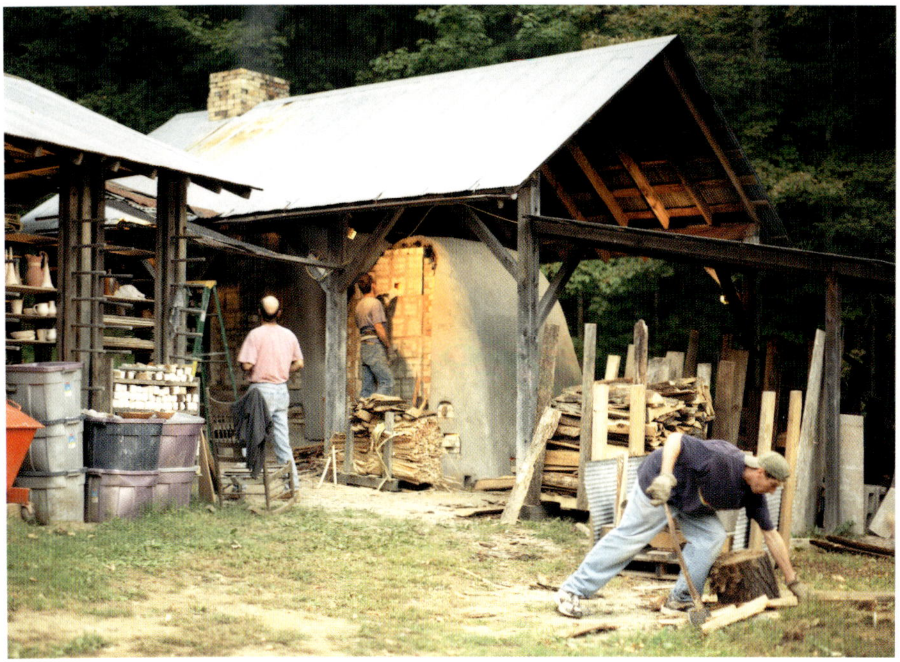

Firing the kiln and checking the spy holes to monitor the heat

the life of a potter. A wood-firing is an arduous process, accomplished by throwing large quantities of pine, birch, and oak into a blazing firebox for fifteen to twenty hours. Several other potters bring their pieces for firing, for it takes a collective effort to keep the fires blazing at the right temperatures.

I asked whether a wood-fired handmade kiln is something of a rarity these days.

"All potters used to build their own kilns. But only a fraction of them do so now, mostly residing in the South. Heat is monitored by looking through spy holes in the kiln at the cones, small ceramic fingers that collapse and melt at successively higher temperatures. Sodium

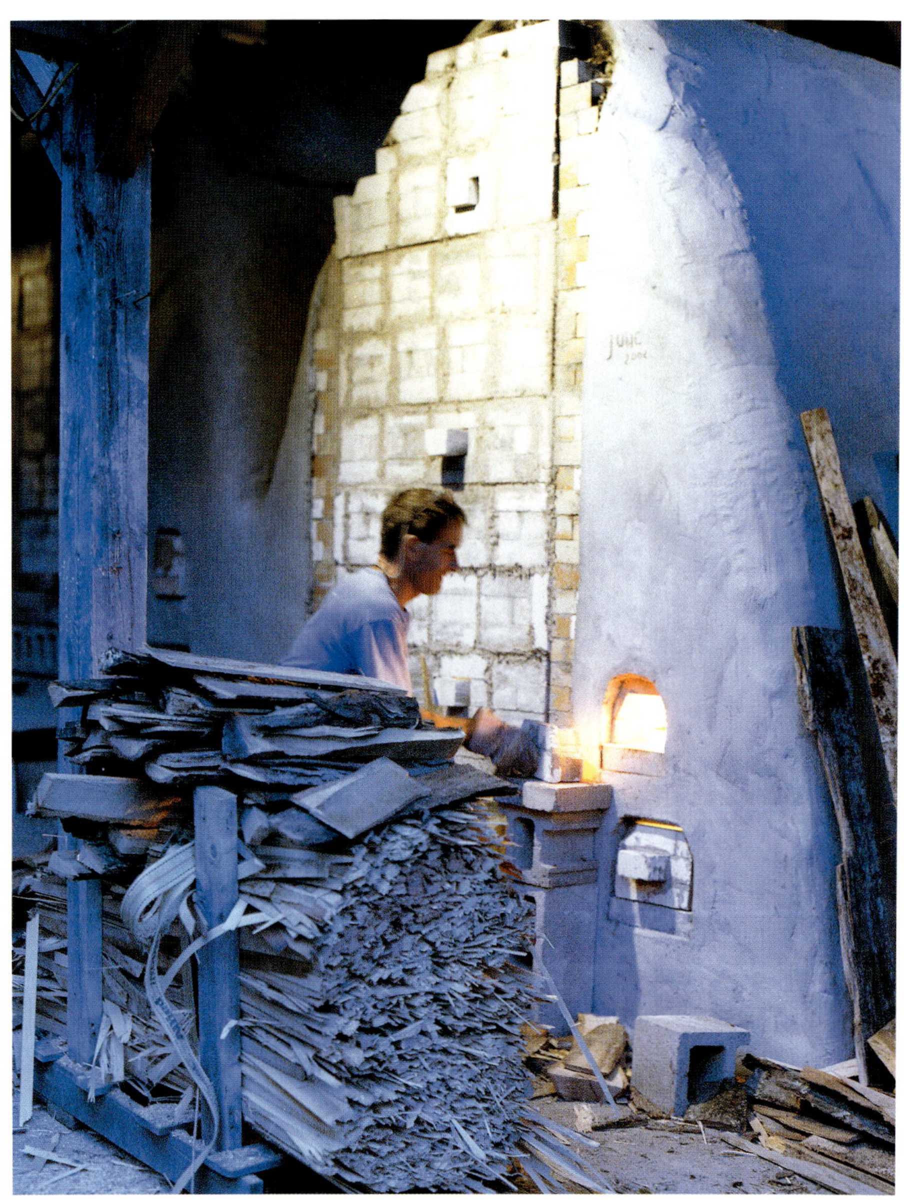

The firing process is long and fatiguing, lasting fifteen to twenty hours.

is added to the kiln, and its vaporization, combined with the pot's proximity to the flames and to the ash produced, create the interesting variations and markings that distinguish the surfaces of wood-fired pots.

"We've seen an increased interest in wood-fired kilns since the late seventies and eighties. Most universities with serious ceramics programs have wood-fired kilns, and in places like North Carolina, a region where a pottery tradition is still of vital importance, wood-fired pottery attracts keen interest.

"You know in the Asian tradition, in Japan for example, great attention is paid to the character of the clay, to the exact region it comes from, its history, its special properties. North Carolina has some of that same interest in continuity and tradition; whole families are devoted to the pottery of their particular region. But unfortunately, except for in the South, in the United States we haven't been careful about retaining the character of our clay, and industrialization has left its mark not only on the earth, but *in* the earth."

Mark shows me multiple plastic cartons filled with a pure clay that has the kinds of properties he favors. Recently he traveled to Maryland to gather the clay from a spot close to the mouth of the Susquehanna River.

In addition to his brisk schedule at the wheel, Mark is in demand as a teacher, offering workshops at such well-known schools as Penland in North Carolina and Haystack School on Deer Isle, Maine. "I like teaching, but I guess I've been rethinking it a lot recently. Often I work and the students watch. But I prefer a model that is more interactive.

"Workshops work best when there's some system of accountability. Often people come to be taught some basic skills in a relatively short period of time and then they're just turned loose. But it takes four to six years of hard work, of making pots every single day, in order to develop the necessary skills, to create a style, a signature for your work. Even though many people think they want to do pottery, they aren't really

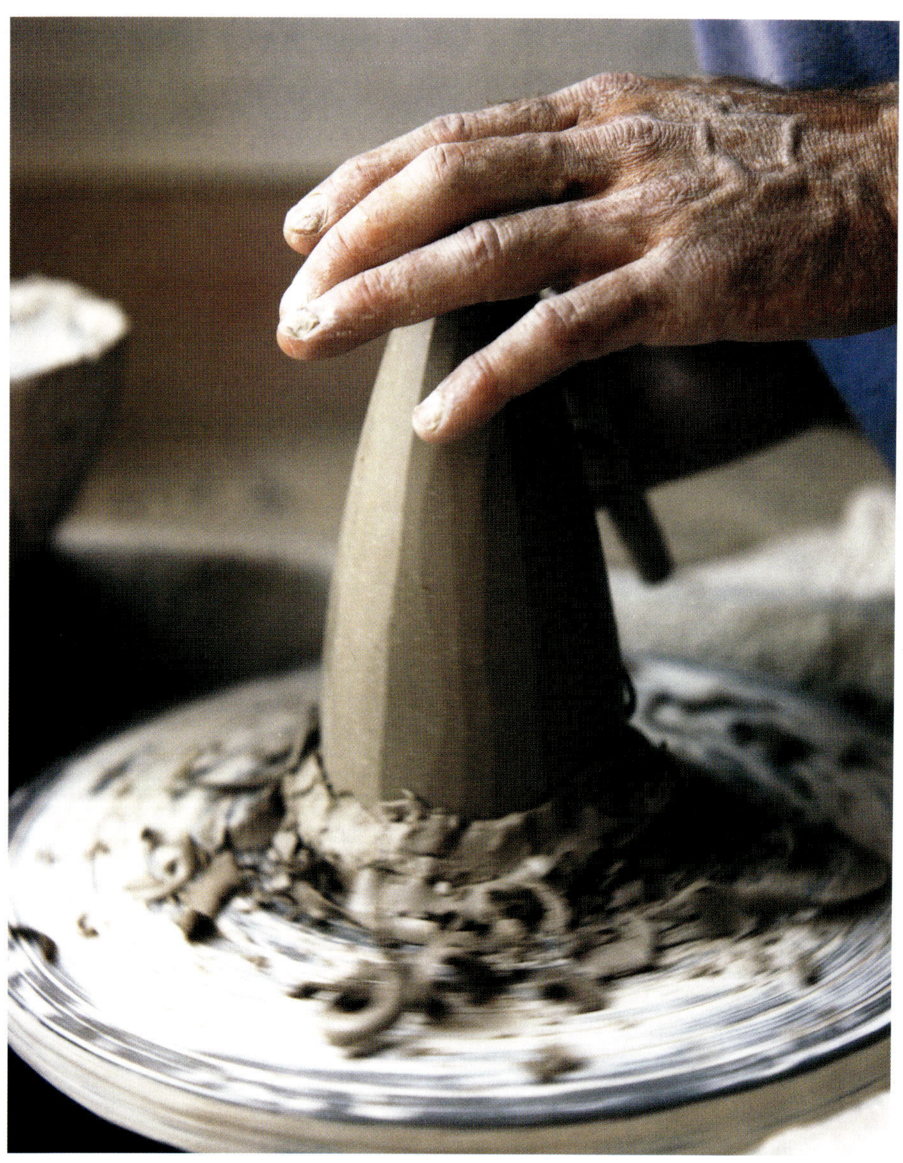

The handmade process: "I am glad just to leave a record of my own touch on this most receptive, fragile, and enduring material."

prepared to make the necessary sacrifices. I think the workshops should be more rigorous, should seek to clarify their purposes, and certainly should convey an honest sense of what it takes to be a good potter."

Although Mark graduated from Amherst College with a degree in anthropology, his interest in making pots dates from grade-school days. "I always liked clay, its plasticity, its spontaneity. It's the ultimate shape-shifter—going from water to stone. I love the engagement with the material.

"I was fortunate enough to attend a private school, the New Lincoln School, in New York City, which encouraged the arts. In fact, most of the teachers were professional artists. And my family, while not artists themselves, respected and supported the arts. So being a potter proba- bly wasn't a 'choice' per se, but rather a journey I embarked on very early. When I think of it, being a potter probably isn't a vocation par- ents can comfortably endorse for a son who needs to make a living. But even though I stopped making pots around the age of sixteen and stud- ied other things in college, I came back to art as if drawn by a magnet.

"I studied sculpture at the University of Massachusetts with Robert Mallory, a sculptor well known in the sixties and seventies as one of the first to experiment with plastics and fiberglass; he was also a pioneer in the study of artificial intelligence. I helped him with several projects and also worked for Michael Singer, an environmental sculptor, installing some of his works, the kind of work that blended into the natural land- scape. Later, I was a workshop studio assistant at Penland School.

"I found that I liked to work with clay more than any of the other mediums. Clay sticks to itself; all other sculpture requires joinery. You're not required to nail, weld, glue, pin, but rather to shape. With clay you can be rather like an athlete in training, learning higher and higher levels of skill and discipline, which result in better and better work.

"I bought this place in 1986 and started out in partnership with [potters] Sam Taylor and Michael Kline. I had the property; the others needed work space and gallery space. Subsequently, they went on to establish their own studios and kilns elsewhere and I acquired a series of apprentices. Though I make every piece I sell myself, my apprentice shares a lot of the labor that goes into the maintenance of a place like this."

From the open kiln area Mark and I can look down on the natural clapboard house. When I remark on its beauty, he laughs, waving a hand dismissively.

"This place was a shipwreck of a house when I bought it, probably the only reason I could afford it. The front part of the house dates from 1790 or so and the ell was probably added in the mid-1800s. I pretty much restored it myself. I did twelve years of carpentry in order to support myself while I was getting my pots out there, my work known. But the house is still a work in progress, and I've found recently that it's more efficient to hire people to do the remaining carpentry. My tools aren't sharp anymore and carpentry requires very specific hand skills. I don't have those hand skills anymore; I've developed the ones required for my pottery. Of course you always retain basic skills, but to execute something really fine you have to practice it and practice it. And you have to be *present* in the work." He taps the side of his head. "Whether in carpentry or pottery, the passion flows from practice and presence."

Mark spoke about the kinds of pottery or traditions that have influenced him the most.

"The pots I most admire, whether great Asian stoneware, old jugs from LaBorne, France, or early American saltware, were made in great quantities by potters who worked every day and who fired large wood-burning kilns. Their work had a purpose, a practical utility, but it also had a power. I think functionality and power are more connected than we sometimes realize."

Mark has grown increasingly visible in recent years as a lecturer on

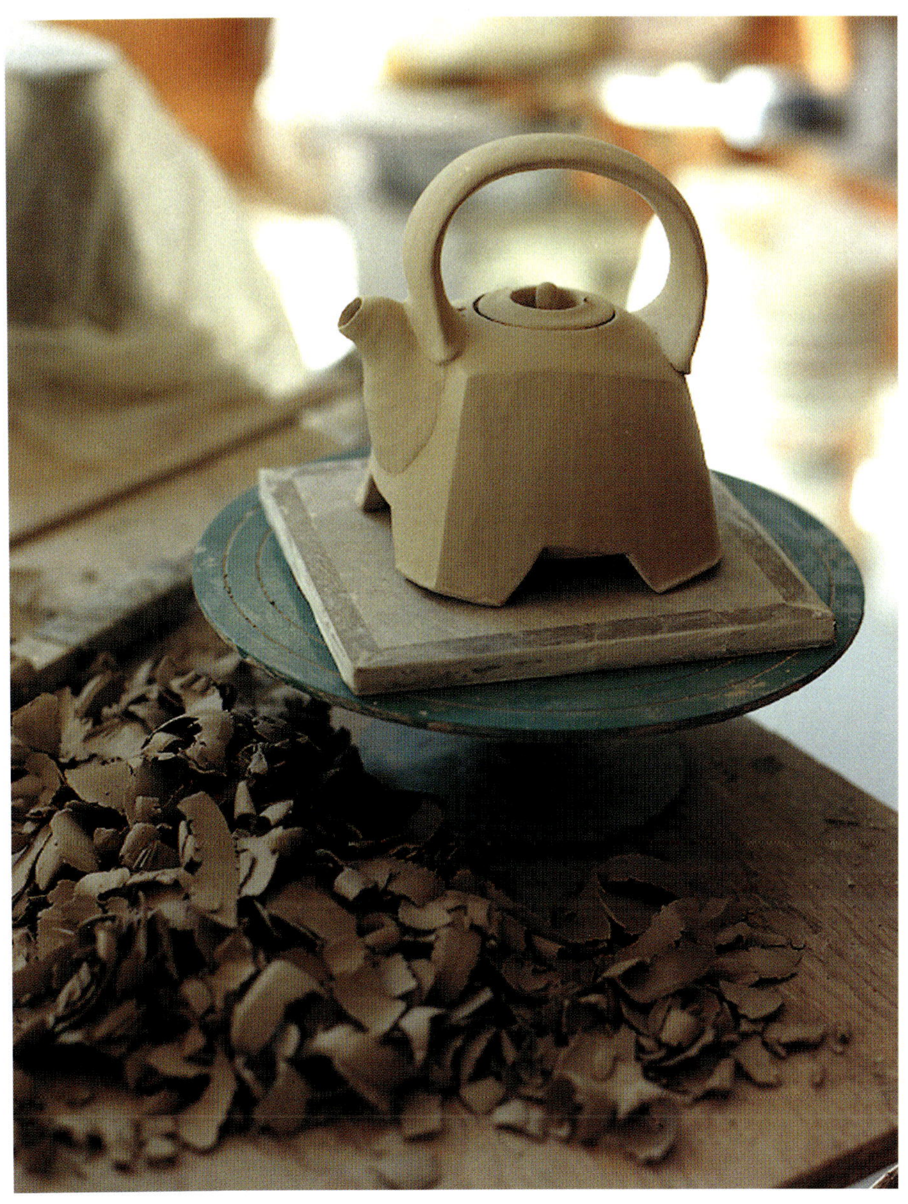

Completed teapot. "I think functionality and power are more connected than we sometimes realize."

early American saltware and as a curator of ceramics shows. At Lacoste Gallery in Concord, Massachusetts, he has curated shows featuring architectural forms (for example, "boxes" whose structures pivot on angles and planes rather than curves or rims), and an exhibit showcasing new potters, called "Fresh Clay." He has participated in several exhibitions curated by Karen Karnes, a Vermont potter whom he holds in special esteem. "She was there at the beginning, when it really counted, at Black Mountain [North Carolina] and Stonypoint [New York], with towering figures in the arts like John Cage and Merce Cunningham. She was there, representing pottery," he says, admiration registering clearly in his voice. "I'd like to write about her work and her enormous influence, just as I'd like to write about some of the new architectural forms and talents I encounter when I curate shows. I'd love to write about my interest in early American stoneware."

I asked Mark—now at the midpoint of his career—whether writing is part of the future he imagines.

"Writing takes time to do well. You have to figure out the trade-offs. Since clay is marginal in the arts world and functional tableware is at the low end of arts purchases, you have to work very hard to make a living. I ask myself why would I make the necessary trade-off in order to write. Apart from wishing to honor Karen Karnes, who has done so much for the pottery world, what else would I want to accomplish? Would I be obsessed with my own reputation, fame? No." He looks me straight in the eye, and I *believe* him. "Do I want to create more opportunities, more space for my work to grow and for people to understand the culture of pottery? Yes. Resoundingly, yes."

En route back to my car I duck into the small building that serves as a gallery for some of Mark's work. A square teapot with four distinctive feet stands beside a jug and several classic pots and jars. While different in size and shape, all of the pieces bear a certain resemblance: spare, unadorned lines, jade and chocolate colors—earth tones all, and the kind of curve or lip that makes you catch your breath. I look back for a moment, expecting to offer a compliment or two. But I can hear Mark speaking with Michael.

"How's that coming?" he inquires. He's going back to work.

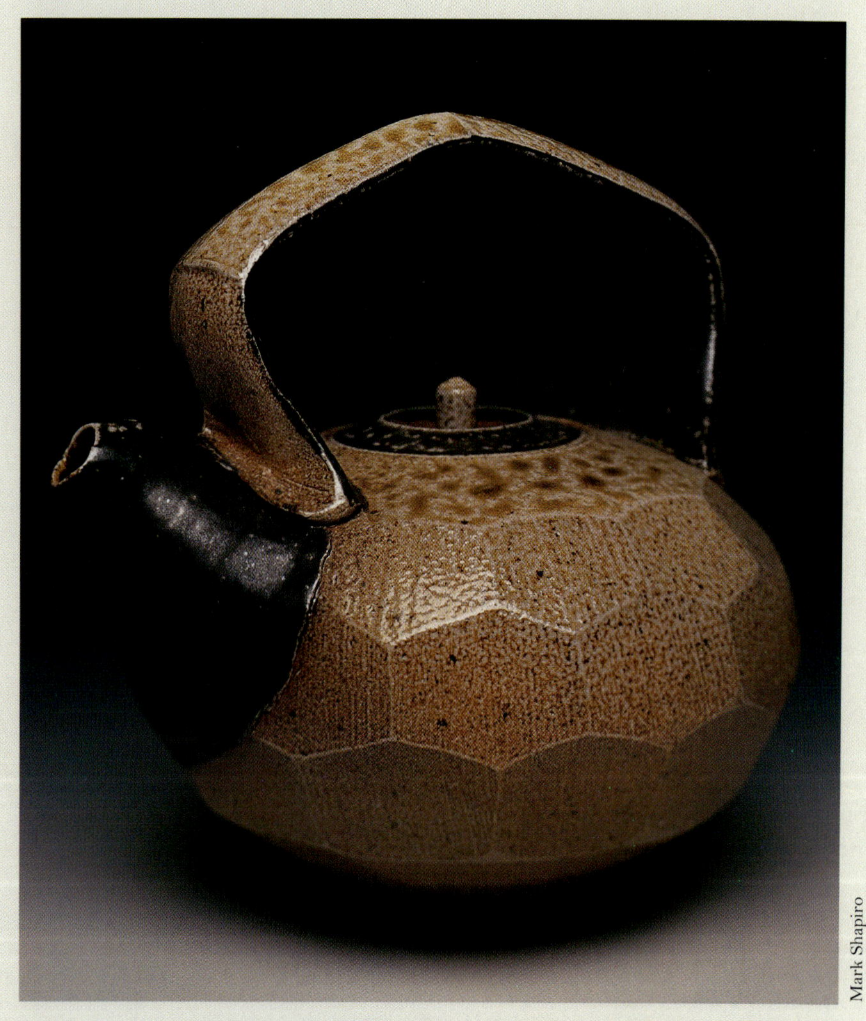

Mark Shapiro

FACETED TEAPOT

8.5" × 8.5" × 7," wood-fired, salt-glazed

"TEAPOTS are the grande dame of functional pots because they require the harmonizing of several separately made parts—the lid, handle, spout, body of the vessel—which all have to work together so the tea can brew properly and pour effortlessly. Teapots also invoke the experience of tea drinking, both in contemporary practice and in historically rich centuries-old traditions. The teapot is a kind of focusing, meditative object associated with conversation or contemplation. As it sits on the table after pouring, or even while it waits to be used on the shelf, it continues to represent all of the associations of its history and current use.

"This teapot has three rows of offset facets carved away from the center of its belly. Its separate parts are emphasized by a black slip-glaze applied to the spout, underside of the handle, outer ring of the lid, and foot. The shape of the arched handle echoes the outlines of the facets. A light deposit of ash and salt glaze shows the effects of the wood fire on the raw clay."

—Mark Shapiro

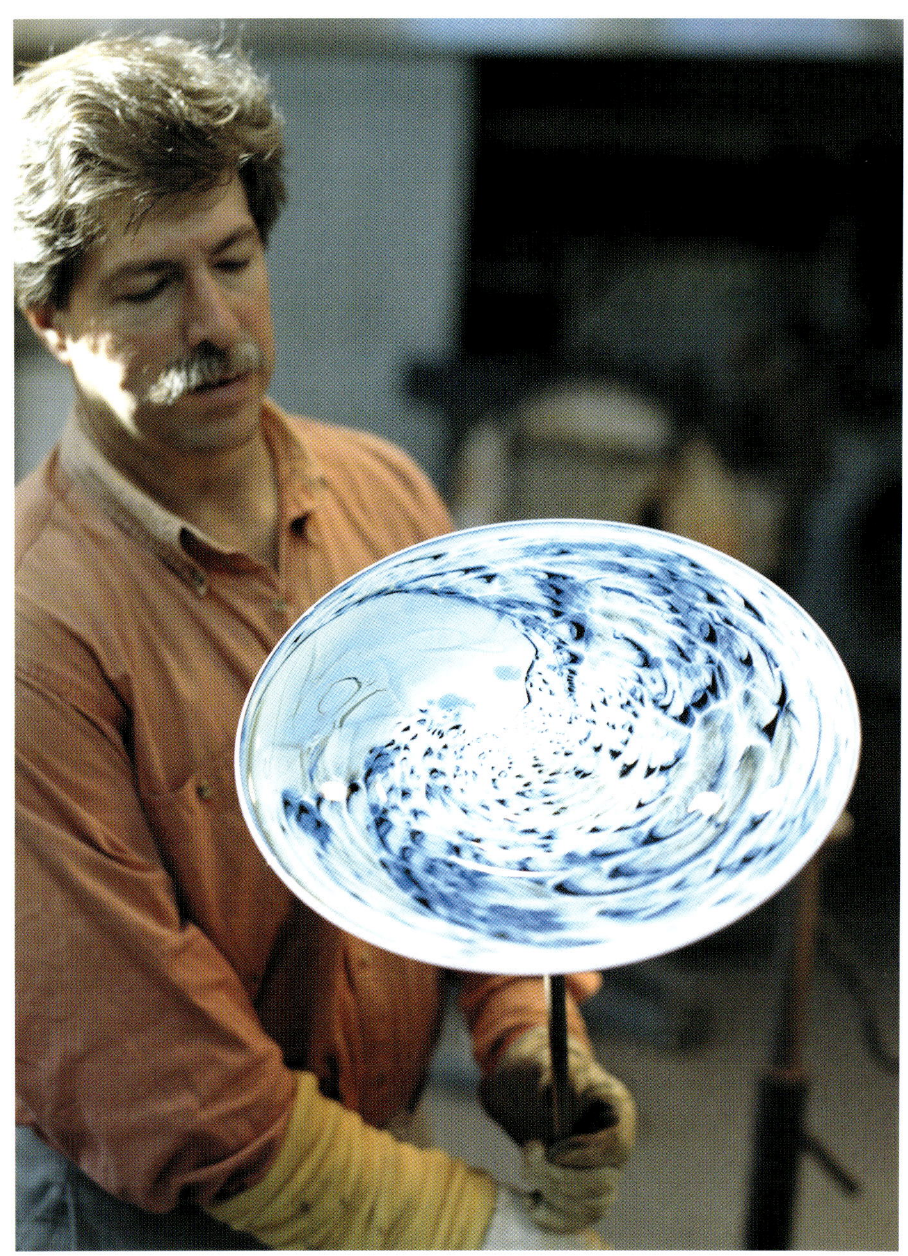

Josh Simpson

JOSH SIMPSON

Artist in Glass

THE MOHAWK TRAIL, that stretch of Route 2 West running from Greenfield to North Adams, rises steeply into the high hill country of Shelburne Falls, the home of Josh Simpson, internationally known artist in glass. To explore Josh's hilltop home, the 1802 post-and-beam house and the immense studio in a converted diary barn, is to move simultaneously backward and forward in time. I visited in mid-September when the front yard maples were just tinged with yellow and when the classic red barn outlined in white trim and the shake-shingle house combined to look like a nineteenth-century New England postcard. But when you enter the realm of Simpson's blown-glass creations—swirling-colored megaplanets, globes that portray what the earth and other planets must look like from outer space, goblets the color of radiation inside a nuclear reactor—you are flying forward into some visionary landscape of the future.

I pull around behind the studio where four or five other cars are parked and am directed to the house by a friendly man who turns out to be one of Josh's assistants. Josh appears at the front door almost immediately; he's been working during the morning hours on wine goblets, something he confides he hasn't made since 1987.

"I'm just beginning to get back into the rhythm again and I'm finding it a real challenge."

Our conversation will take place over lunch, after which I've been invited to tour the studio and watch a portion of the afternoon work session. As he and I set the table, I can't help but remark on the gorgeous ruby glass plates that will hold our sandwiches and the shimmery, paper-thin tumblers that will hold our soft drinks. "That's just what I made to eat and drink from," says the man whose glass is in the White House, smiling out from under a shock of brown hair. Compactly built, Josh has what one of his assistants calls "the arms of a glass-blower," the bulging triceps required to delicately balance pieces of molten glass weighing up to seventy-five pounds at the end of a five-foot metal blowpipe. He also has a moustache worthy of a barbershop baritone and a distinctive walk—a graceful glide, his feet seeming to skim over the floor's surface. Later, when I see him working the glass in the studio, traveling from furnace to bench, to the reheating furnace called "the glory hole" to bench, I see the value of gliding.

"Like many artists who moved into this area twenty-five years ago, I came for several very pragmatic reasons. My ex-wife was completing her Ph.D. in anthropology at the time, I was working at a small studio in Connecticut, and she found a program at the University of Massachusetts that excited her. So we drew a fifty-mile circle around UMass and started to look for a place that would be appropriate for me to work. We weren't even looking for a house at that point.

"I almost bought an old stone church in North Adams, but it didn't have any land associated with it and the only logical place to put the furnaces was where the pulpit used to be. Hellfire in the pulpit didn't seem quite right.

"So we happened upon this idyllic hilltop." He points to the multiple-mile views on three sides of the house. "We could buy enough land for a garden, the barn was large, and the house came with it, totally unexpectedly."

When I remark on the beauty of the house, he adds quickly, "You're seeing it after twenty-five years of improvements. When I first moved in, it was pretty run down. I had a piece of foam rubber for a mattress and one lawn chair."

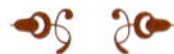

I had heard the story, something of a legend in the Valley, of how Josh Simpson had left Hamilton College at the end of his junior year and traveled to experimental Goddard College hoping to find a glass-blowing program. When he found none, he and several other students at Goddard interested in glass built a furnace from recycled bricks, and Josh set himself up, Thoreauvean style, in a tepee in the Vermont woods. There he lived for a year, heating the space with a wood stove, depending on chickpeas as a major source of protein, and developing his style and technique as a glassblower.

"Actually, I was amazingly happy in my tepee. I still have it out in the barn. I feel there may come a time when the guys from the bank show up and say, 'Sorry, buddy; you're outta here.' That's when it's good to have a tepee.

"And it still amazes me that I could buy all of this [he sweeps his arms around in the air] for $57,000, and in the bargain inherit all there is about New England that makes it New England: twisting roads, breathtaking views, miles of snaking stone walls, neighbors, and a community of artists who permit privacy or community at whatever rate you want to access it.

"You know, craftspeople have this odd rhythm to our lives. Much of what we do every day is introspective, solitary work. And now and then you come out—say to the American Crafts Festival, or the Paradise City Arts Festival. And you see old friends and make new contacts, or think about new techniques or how to build new equipment —there's all that cross-fertilization. And then it's back to solitary again."

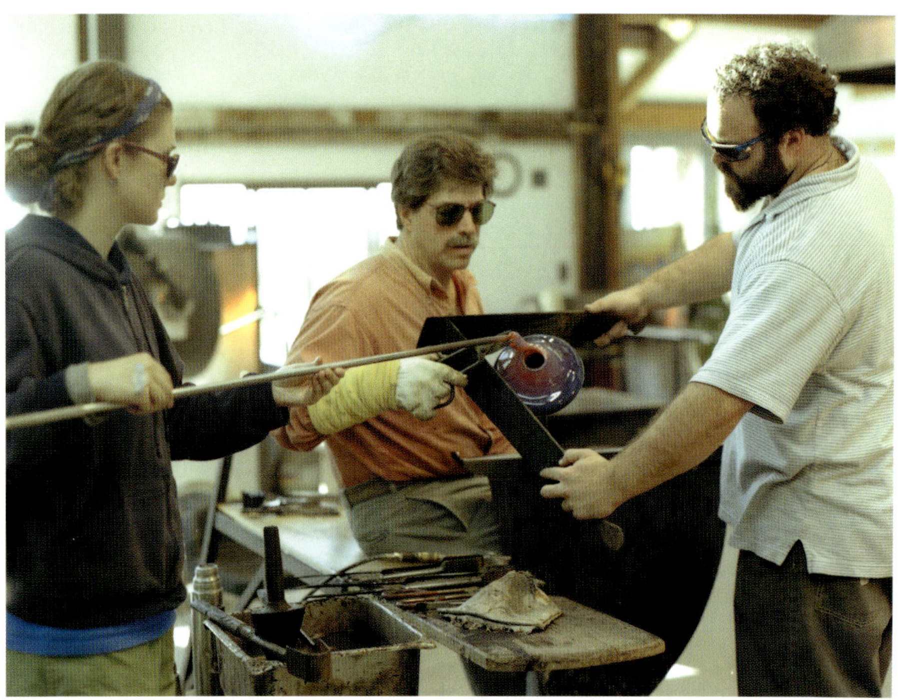

Water-soaked pieces of wood are used as shaping and supportive tools when working with molten glass.

Thinking about the number of cars out by the studio, I asked Josh if he worked with apprentices.

"Actually, I worked entirely alone for six years, never seeking an apprentice. But I got one anyway. One evening when I was still at the Connecticut studio, a young guy drove in on a motorcycle: Chris Constantine was his name and he had ridden all the way from New Orleans. He had seen some of my glass and decided he wanted to work for me. Well, I told him I didn't have a job for him, but there he was with this oil stripe all the way up his back where the chain had thrown up oil over the course of a thousand-mile ride. So of course I had to put him up for the night. And he never left. We worked together for almost six years, through the move up here, until he and his wife, Kathy, opened their own studio in Shelburne Falls.

"After working with Chris, I realized I could delegate other responsibilities to others. At first my apprentices didn't blow glass at all—but now the nature of what I do has become so complex, uses so many different things and takes so much preparation, that they assist me with everything I do. My crew and I thrive on each other's energy and enthusiasm and that creates a wonderful spirit in the studio.

"I vary my projects so that I won't become bored with the repetition of making one thing over and over. Sometimes something spontaneous happens that makes me turn to a specific project. For example, when I was first digging a garden outside our kitchen area here, I came upon a number of glass marbles, left who knows when by kids playing generations ago. I was struck by how durable glass is, how it survives—buried in the earth—for sometimes hundreds or perhaps thousands of years. Since no museum at that time, in 1976, was collecting my work, I decided I'd create my own legacy: I'd create little minature spheres, miniplanets, and bury them or place them in out-of-the-way places all around the country and around the world. I've made thousands of these little spheres and now have something called the Infinity Project where anybody can write to my Web site and request a planet, telling me where they'd like to place it and why. If I like their story I send them two: one to keep and the other to place."

Josh spoke about the skills required to become an artist in glass and how he managed to train himself.

"There was a master's program in glass at Alfred University I kind of wanted to get into. I got accepted, but the tuition was $1,400 a semester, and even with a job, I didn't have that kind of money. So I learned the craft myself. I read a lot about the history of glass, but more important, I went to look at glass at the Corning Glass Museum and

the Metropolitan Museum in New York City. I studied their glass and
I asked myself, 'How can I make that?' I learned skills by trying.

"I equate glassblowing to dancing. I know that sounds kind of
strange. But if you watch ballet, or Celtic dance, or clogging, or even
square dancing, you can see that there are quite specific steps, that they
are done precisely and oftentimes incredibly quickly. So fast that the
dancer can't think: *step one forward, tap, tap, tap, jump, jump, step back.* It's
not something your conscious mind is reasoning its way through.

"It's the same thing with glassblowing. There are specific steps,
quite precisely executed, and sometimes you have to move very quickly,
but the movement comes from body memory. Glassblowing is sense
memory, kind of like what string or wind musicians call finger memory.
When I was learning to fly airplanes, I had a terrible time letting go of
all the conscious steps, particularly when practicing landing. Then I
figured out that flying was like dancing or glassblowing. I needed to let
my body instinctively react. Of course this didn't dawn on me until after four hundred landings."

I told Josh he seemed to be someone who, when he sets out to do
something, however challenging, simply *does* it.

"Yes, that's honestly the way I work," he responded. "I think it
may be the function of testosterone poisoning, that core belief that
you can figure out how to do just about everything you set your mind
to. I don't know why I possess that confidence. It's certainly led me to
take on massive and insane projects. And I don't mean to sound arro-
gant about this. I realize my own limitations in terms of education,
expertise, sheer physical strength. But if I believe I can do it, many
times I can.

"Here's an example." He grabs a group of photographs from a side
table. One image shows a giant propane gas tank, fifty feet long and
about eleven feet in diameter, being lowered into an enormous hole by
what Josh calls "the biggest crane in New England." Josh and his crew

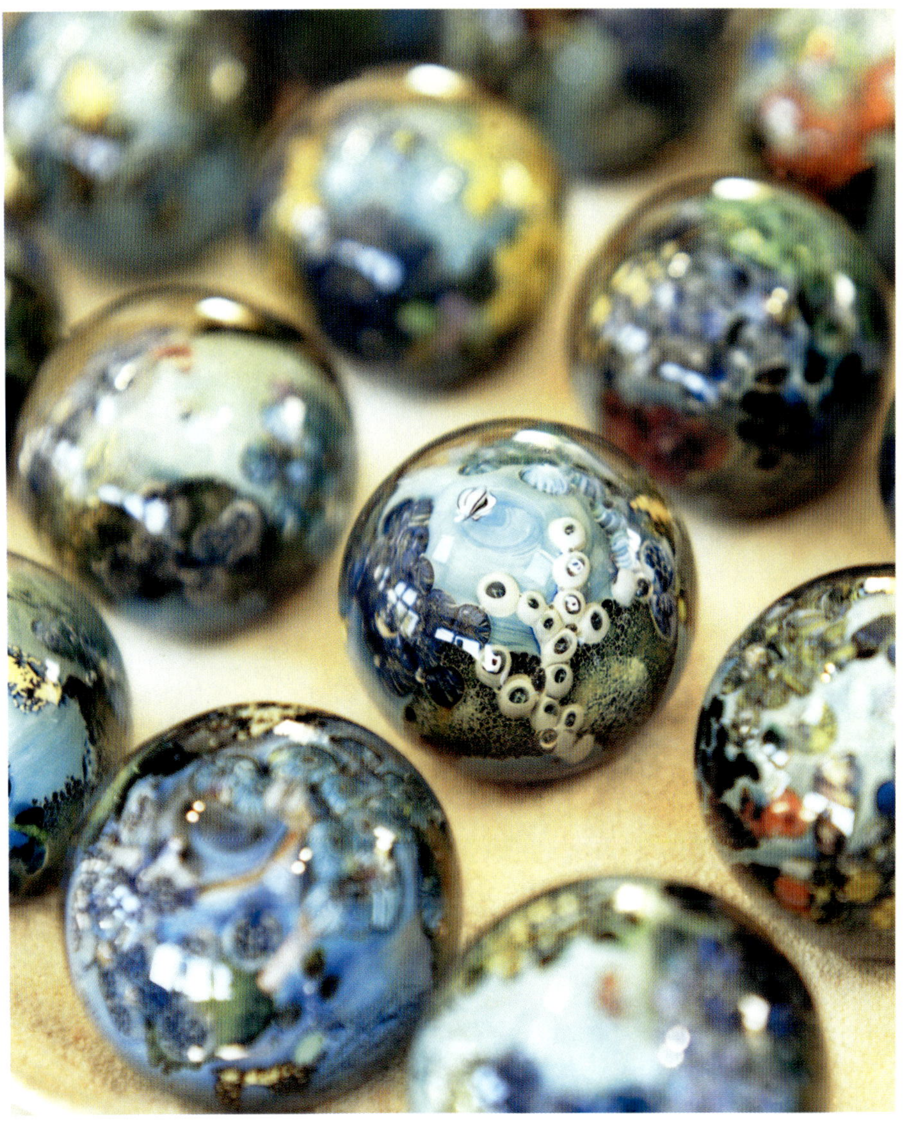

Finished "planets." The "inner worlds" of the planets are created by rolling the first "gather" in crushed glass filaments before adding another gather of molten glass.

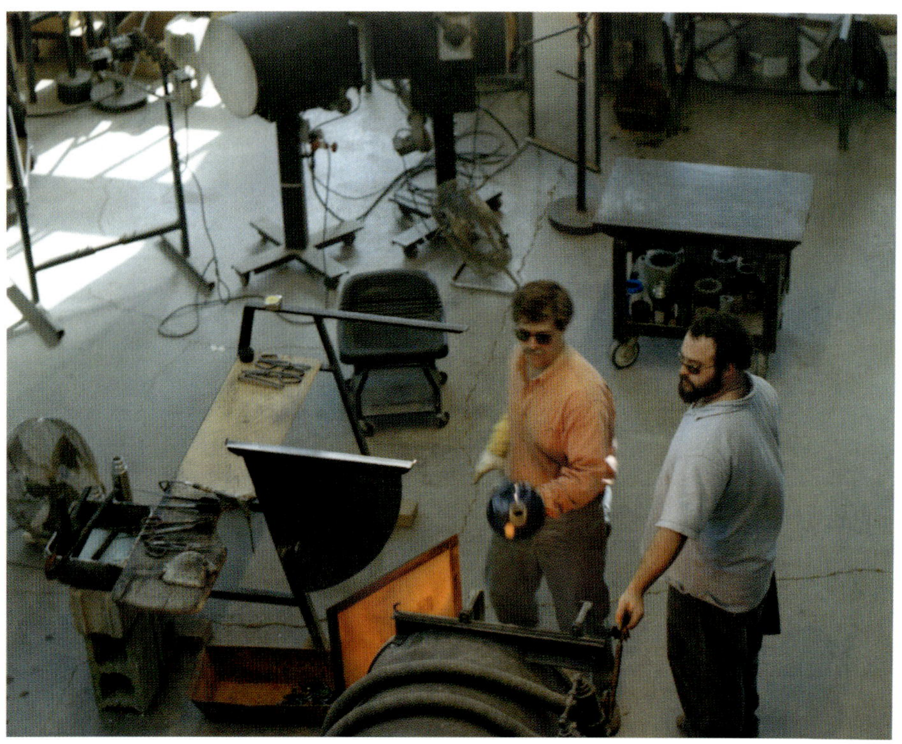

A converted dairy barn, which serves as Josh Simpson's "hot shop." Josh and his assistants make all the furnaces and equipment used in the studio. Josh wears heat-resistant gloves, and he and his assistants wear sunglasses to protect against damage from the intense heat.

members are standing jubilantly beside the behemoth, looking like tiny tin soldiers.

"I use propane gas in all my furnaces, and if you buy propane in quantity it costs less. I used to have three 1,000-gallon tanks buried on the property. Little submarines. But a year ago I broke my leg and had nothing to do for eight weeks. So I decided I'd look for a bigger tank." At this point we both start chuckling.

"I found a 30,000-gallon tank in Mashpee on the Cape, so then I had the challenge and the fun of getting it here, buried, connected, welded up. I wanted to do the welding myself until I found out you had to have a special license in Massachusetts." He looks at the pictures with undisguised glee. Beneath the pictures of the tank are shots of a similarly gleeful two-year-old, Josh's son Jamey, who is strapped into the seat of Josh's Piper Comanche. Although Josh uses commercial jets to "commute" to see his wife, Cady, a Space Shuttle astronaut for NASA in Houston, he and his family use the Comanche to travel all over the East Coast. "Jamey's a veteran flyer," he says with a quick nod of satisfaction.

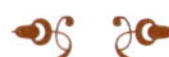

Christina Emery, one of the studio assistants, comes to give a tour of the studio while Josh prepares for his afternoon work session. We climb to the second story of the barn where hundreds of glass rods in every conceivable color are stored. From rods like these, along with a mélange of metallic oxides, Josh will make his "formulas," the mix of colors that makes his work distinctive. Here the completed glass objects are stored and mailed all over the world. Finally we come to a balcony overlooking the studio floor. From this vantage point the four furnaces are clearly visible; they melt the glass to a point where it takes on, as Christina terms it, "the consistency of warm honey." Across from the furnaces is Josh's bench, a wooden seat with horizontal metal arms on either side where he rests and rolls the blowpipe, turning the glass and trimming away excess. Assistants have benches at the far end of the studio close to the kilns, which cool the finished glass slowly enough that it does not develop cracks. The assistants appear to be making the tiny planets used in the Infinity Project.

Once downstairs, Christina positions me about ten feet directly behind Josh. He begins to work. Josh dips the end of the blowpipe into

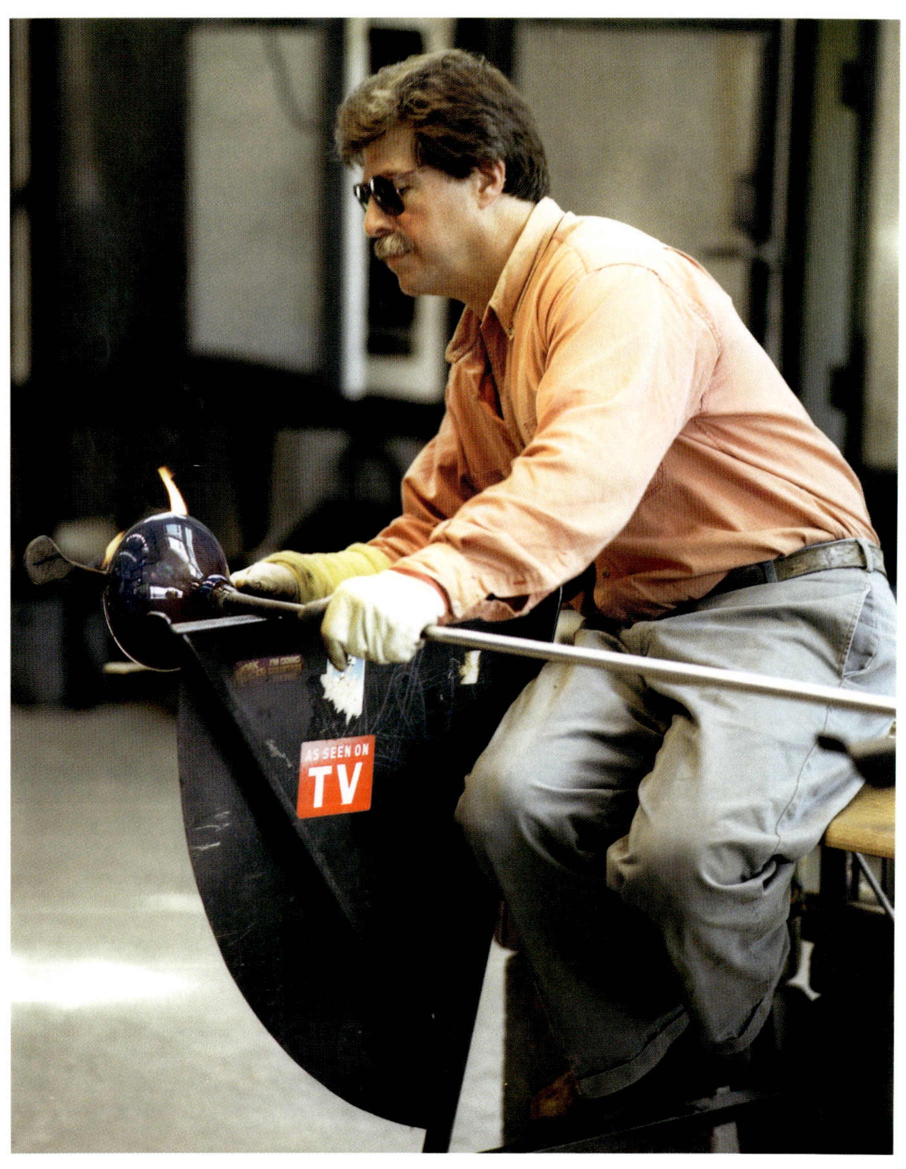

Josh, working at his bench. To keep molten glass from distorting under its own weight, Josh rotates the blowpipe as he shapes the piece.

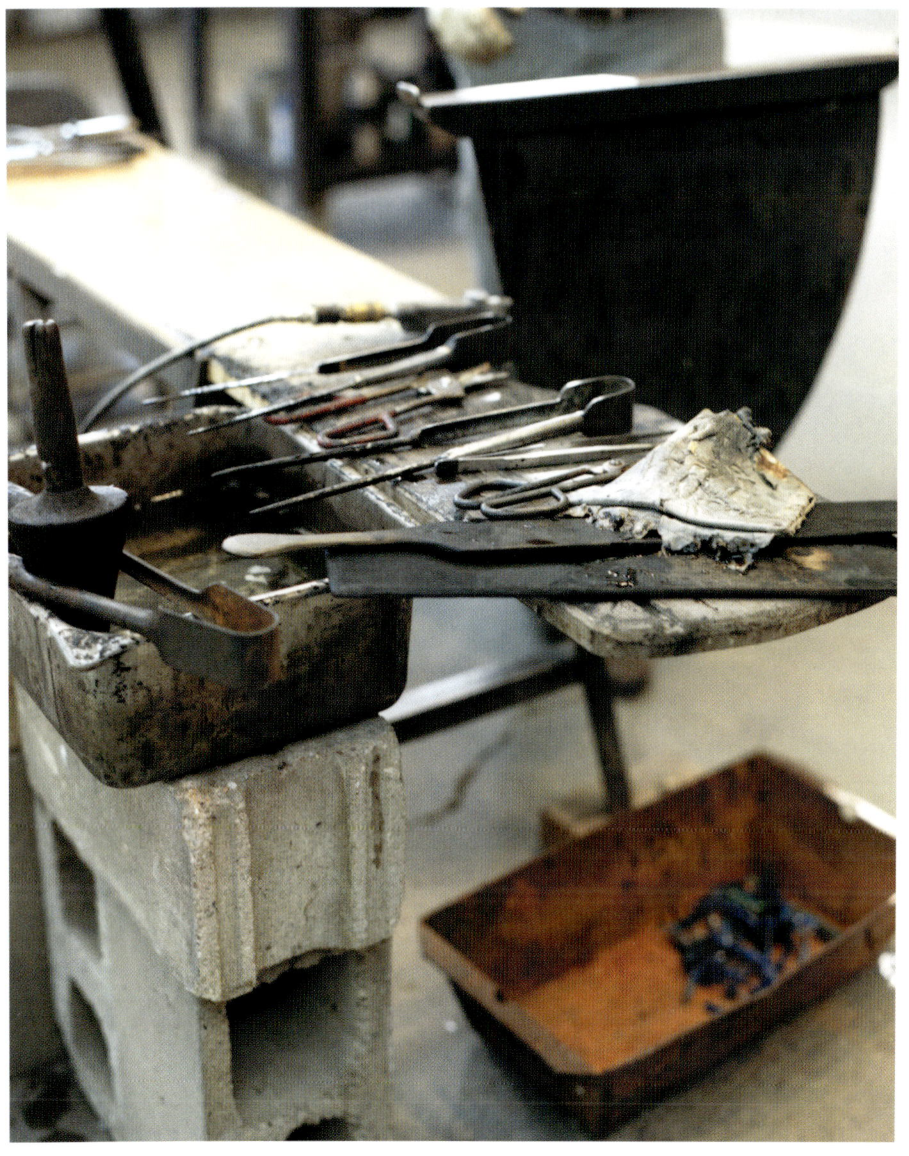

The tools of an artist in glass

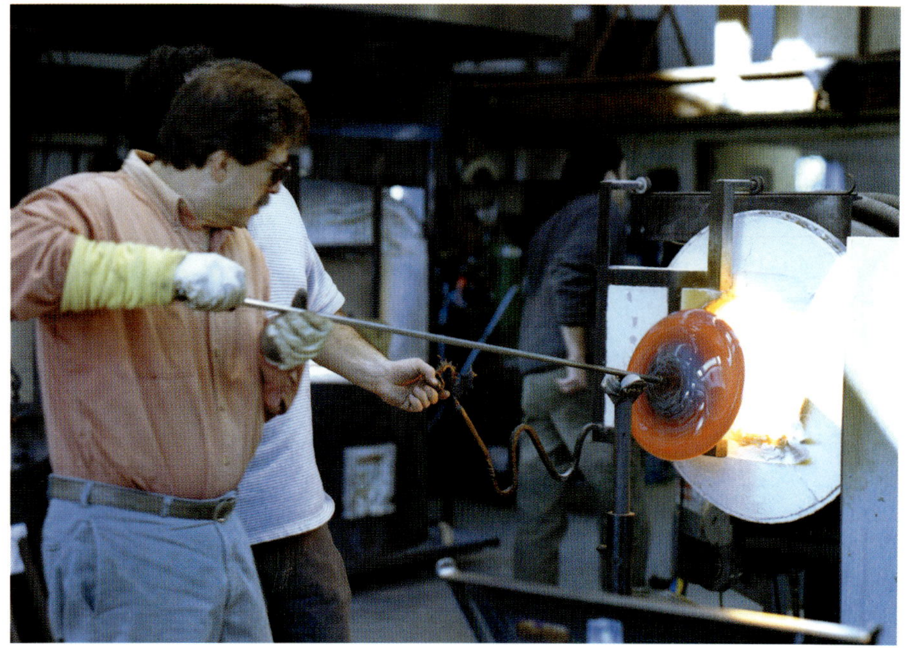

Reheating a piece in the "glory hole," the furnace used to reheat cooling glass for further working

molten glass in the furnace, pulling it out and shaping the blob into a sphere. He returns to his bench area and blows; as the sphere elongates, he twists the blowpipe and quickly assumes his seat, rolling the pipe slowly on the metal rests as the stem of the goblet emerges. A wooden shaping tool, soaked in water, is applied to create the goblet's base. Music is playing in the background, and Josh's body positions and movements are decisive and at the same time completely fluid.

There's almost too much to see, and as I glance away to watch an assistant completing a miniplanet, I miss the fact that Josh's goblet is complete, ready to be transferred to the cooling kiln. He repeats this process four, five, six times, and each time the emergence of the silver blue goblet (its color created by melting silver metal in the glass), exquisitely shaped, seems like some alchemist's illusion. The perfect magic trick.

I know not to interrupt the work session, so I wave good-bye as Josh is blowing his eighth goblet. Climbing upstairs to the back exit, I focus on something carefully stacked in the eaves of the barn. It appears to be a number of long, tapered, apparently hand-carved poles lashed together: Josh's tepee.

SET OF RUBY GOBLETS

9" tall

"BLOWING GOBLETS MARKED the beginning of my serious commitment to this craft, my earliest training in the intricate and delicate skills necessary to be successful as a glass artist. Goblets present real technical challenges; they require the ability to blow a delicately crafted bowl balanced on an incredibly thin stem and foot. For some reason, people expect to buy them in sets, where, ideally, one must look very like the other. I might never have tried them, except for the confluence of certain things.

"I began to work in glass in 1971. This was the time I was living in my tepee, with virtually no money and very rudimentary tools and equipment. There was a health foods store in town, and they wanted my partner Bob Burch and me to make goblets as ice cream dishes, containers to be used at their soda fountain. I could trade my goblets for a food credit—so, suddenly, I had a compelling reason to blow goblets. Goblets translated into fifty-pound bags of chickpeas and broken bits of sharp cheddar cheese.

"Making goblets over and over again began to refine my techniques. I began to realize how tiny changes could radically affect the outcome. Just how I performed the first gather, a tiny bit more air in my blowpipe, or one awkward movement or moment of inattention could result in disaster. So even though goblets began as my ticket to survival, gradually they became a kind of proving ground for my art, teaching me the finesse, the grace, the technique necessary to make art glass."

—Josh Simpson

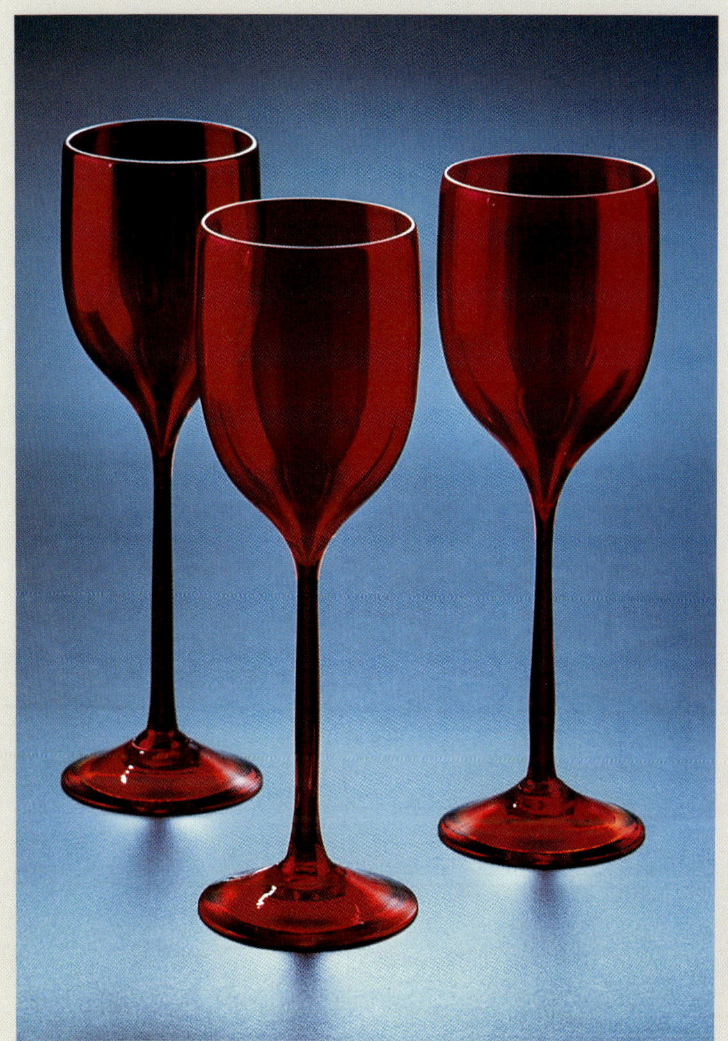

Tommy Olof Elder

❧ FIBER ARTS ❧

QUILTS affording basic warmth but also decorated with original and inventive designs appeared all over colonial America. Sometimes they originated from pure necessity, sometimes as a showcase for a housewife's skill with a needle and thread. Appliquéd quilts (stitched to a foundation cloth), pieced quilts (assembled blocks of fabric strips), or quilts made of whole pieces of cloth became prize possessions of many families. Examples are preserved in colonial American museums such as those in Historic Deerfield Village. Memorial Hall Museum in Old Deerfield is one of New England's oldest historical museums and houses an extraordinary collection of textiles as well as furnishings, paintings, and Indian artifacts, some dating from the 1600s. Here a vistor can see varied examples of piecework that demonstrate the rich and diverse heritage of quilt making in this country. One of the most remarkable quilts in the Old Deerfield collection is one composed of stars, hexagons, and polygons, made by "Mrs. Carpenter of Vermont." The quilt, made around 1860, is created out of tiny diamond-shaped pieces of calico; approximately 82,000 individual pieces create the complex patterns. Contemporary quilters have been asked to respond to the patterns, fabrics, colors, and quilting of this intricate piece by participating in the "Old Deerfield Quilt Challenge" and have produced innovative interpretations of their own.

A number of quilting traditions and techniques are enjoying new and enthusiastic interest, the consequence of a major quilting revival over the past twenty years. "Crazy quilts," a parlor craft practiced by women in the nineteenth century, are constructed from valuable bits of saved fabric like silk or velvet that are then sewn into ornate "throws," often showcasing the needlework of a particular quilter. Amish quilts featuring bold, deep colors and geometric designs seem, almost paradoxically, to resemble twentieth-century minimalist paintings. Album or story quilts, made to commemorate a special occasion or to be a gift for a parting friend, are composed of individual squares, each depicting a picture of special significance and each contributing to the "narrative" of the whole. "Samplers" are also a part of quilt and sewing traditions; many feature intricate stitching, alphabets, quotations, maps, genealogies. In the Pioneer Valley, the growing interest in and enthusiasm for fiber arts is evidenced in a new exhibition, retail, and educational center located in downtown Amherst and in "Hands Across the Valley," a huge and hugely diverse invitational quilt show mounted each spring at Amherst College.

A study of many of these traditions informs the quilts of Susan Boss and Mark Brown. Combining Boss's expert sewing with Brown's training as a painter and designer, this husband-and-wife team create bold and arresting quilts grounded in the techniques, images, and sewing expertise revered in the folk art tradition. Often beginning at the center of a piece and building organically outward, their quilts use some of the images of flowers, trees, stars, and birds or quotations chosen from poems that one might find in traditional quilts; yet these are embedded within a surprisingly modern mix of colors and fabrics. Their quilts carry the warmth of tradition and the shock of the modern, each enhancing the other.

Sally Dillon's love affair with silk and her return to her New England roots coincided serendipitously with Northampton's two-year celebration of its once-booming silk industry. Samuel Whitmarsh, a Boston-born businessman, began the "boom" in 1832 by planting twenty-five acres of mulberry trees in the Florence section of Northampton and building a large cocoonery for the silk worms. When his business faltered, the mill was taken over briefly by the Northampton Association for Education and Industry, a utopian community of reformers and abolitionists—including, famously, Sojourner Truth. After the commune dissolved, Sam Hill, one of its members who invented a machine capable of twisting silk into thread, established (with the support of the Singer Sewing Machine Company) the Nonotuck Silk Company. This company later became the Corticelli Silk Company, which grew into one of the world's largest producers of thread. Dillon designed a shimmering silk "story quilt" for the celebration, featuring intricate hand-painted images culled from the high points of the city's history of silk production, stretching from 1832 to 1930. Acknowledging silk's beauty is central to all of Dillon's work, whether she is painting, dyeing, and designing "story quilts" depicting New England landscapes, nature preserves, and ecology, or constructing unique yet functional silk jackets and scarves.

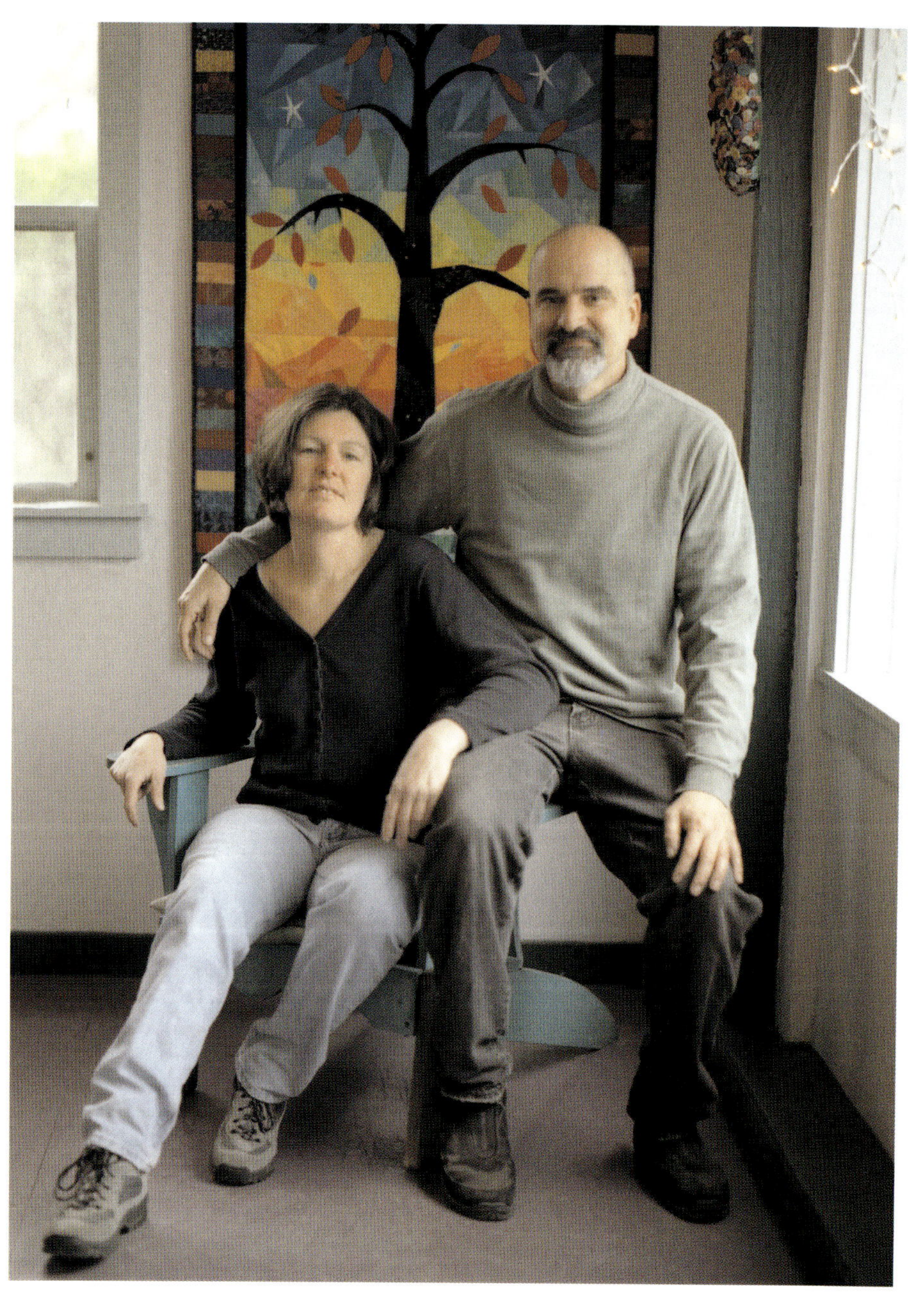

Susan Boss and Mark Brown

SUSAN BOSS AND MARK BROWN

Makers of Folk Art Quilts

Susan Boss and Mark Brown, a husband-and-wife team, have been engaged for the past twenty years in making striking folk art quilts featuring bold colors and unpredictable design elements. They work in a renovated barn just yards from their home in Easthampton. They purchased the home primarily because it had a history as a "working house," serving in years past as a bakery with a large barn for the horses and bakery wagons necessary for sales deliveries. Gradually, they renovated the house, removing large ovens from the basement and reconstructing that space to house their silk-screening operation. The barn was then converted into double studio space. The dowstairs level provides the work space for drawing the patterns on paper, altering them, discussing their size and composition, and preparing the drawings for silk screens. The second floor is devoted to Mark's other artwork, the making of clocks and metal sculptures. The studio, painted a mint green, is an open and airy space dotted with wide windows and big flat-topped worktables.

Patterns hang on the walls: a tree of life, a giant sunflower, an open hand with a heart embedded in it. An oak "card catalog," probably discarded from a library when computerized systems replaced its hands-on filing system, stands close to the entryway. Each drawer opens to

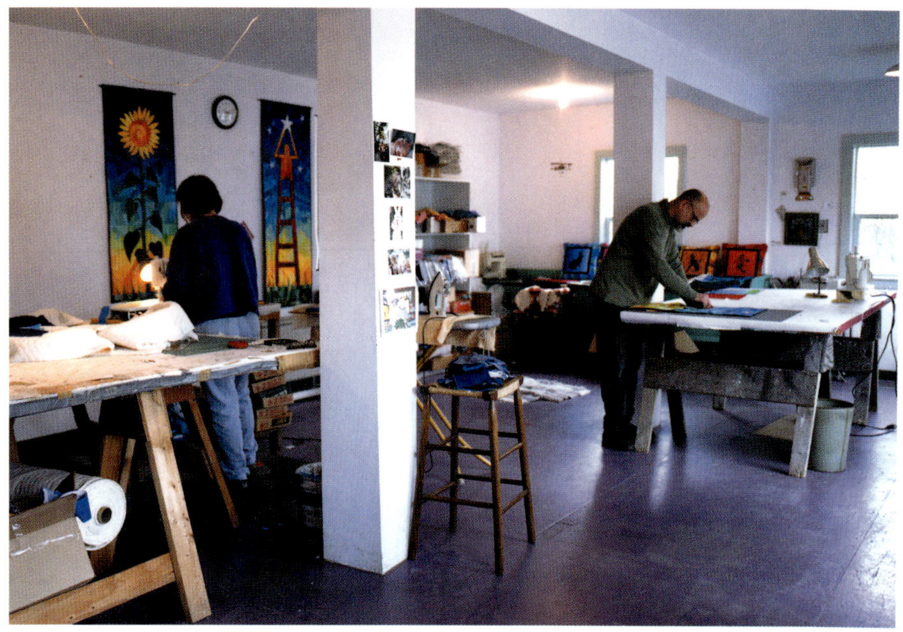

Mark and Susan's downstairs studio space in the converted barn. "We work well together as a team."

reveal a letter of the alphabet silk-screened on brightly colored fabric. These letters, drawn and printed by Mark, sometimes make their way into quotations sewn into a quilt's design. Photographs of several quilts command attention. One in particular, a vertical quilt bordered by strips of fabric in alternating colors, depicts a graceful tree bearing red leaves, its trunk rooted in the earth, yet reaching to the stars. We sit at one of the worktables for our three-way conversation. Susan speaks rapidly, often infusing her comments with a ready laugh; Mark likes to ponder the question. Yet it becomes clear very quickly that they speak and work as a collaborative unit, one long accustomed to an intricate and integrated dance.

Susan leans forward, beginning the conversation:

"My family—and it's a large one since I am the oldest of ten children—grew up in the Springfield area. My father, his father, and one of my brothers became doctors. Although I was the first person in my family to step out as an artist, later my sister Shelia became a visual artist and my brothers Chris and Tom became musicians, though they both have 'day jobs.'

"I think I knew very early that I was creative. In fact, I remember clearly my earliest money-making scheme. In the fourth grade I invited the neighborhood kids to a crafts class in my basement at fifty cents an hour. Given the fact that it was a rock-bottom price and I was good with kids, I was quite successful. I was hooked. I studied weaving at the Rochester Institute of Technology for a time after high school. And when I was nineteen I took a quilting course at the Brookfield Crafts Center; I have quilted ever since. For a time, while living on Cape Cod, I began to teach quilting in my home. I read books about the process and experimented with new techniques and patterns. With another quilter I opened a business to buy, sell, and make quilts. Since I had two small children by that time, I also began to repair quilts that people brought into the store. This was perhaps my most instructive experience, as it allowed me to examine how other people had structured their quilts many, many years ago.

"When I returned to Western Massachusetts to work on my B.F.A. at the University of Massachusetts, I taught quilt making at the Hill Institute in Florence. I also studied painting—and I was lucky to study with professors who took a very broad view of that medium, allowing me to create pieces that blended fabric, ornamentation, design.

"In 1978 I was in a serious automobile accident: I was riding my bicycle towards an intersection and a woman, who didn't see me, made a sudden left-hand turn—running right into me. I shattered my femur. Although I was fortunate not to have sustained a serious head or spine injury, I was in traction for many weeks and doctors told me I'd always walk with a limp. I thought to myself while lying there, *Oh, no, I won't,* and when I moved into the rehabilitation process I taught myself how to roller-skate. I simply kept my sneaker skates on all day, every day for a couple of weeks. Soon I was comfortable skating everywhere. I skated for recovery and for fun with my kids, and gradually, also as a form of art. I made a harness and giant fabric wings and became known as the "butterfly lady," skating through Northampton and the smaller, outlying towns, a kind of performance artist. I can remember my mother watching this whole process and saying with some incredulity, "Are you going to roller-skate until you become a grandmother?" And of course, I wasn't. But when you think about it, it had a lot going for it: It was improvisational—rather than waiting for customers to seek me out, I could chase the customers; it was entertaining for my kids, Jen and Dylan, who often had costumes too and would create a little improvisational piece in my routine. You know, I still have my wings."

"And people still come up to you on the street and say, 'Aren't you the butterfly lady?'" Mark breaks in, and scrambles to find a photo album. There is a picture of the "butterfly lady," looking at ease on her skates while supporting huge diaphanous wings. They both chuckle at the memories and Mark settles back, his feet propped against the worktable, ready to pick up his narrative.

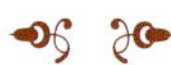

"I was born and raised in south Georgia and I think, like Susan, I always knew I would become an artist. I began as a painter and came to the University of Massachusetts in the mid-seventies to get an M.F.A. Clearly, there were many more opportunities in the fine arts in New England and, as luck would have it, the first person I met in Massachusetts was Mark Shapiro.

I asked if he meant Mark Shapiro, the potter (who is also profiled in this book).

"The very same." He laughs, adding quickly, "Small world. Mark and I shared an apartment for four years while he was a student at Amherst College. In fact, we shared studio space in Northampton from 1979 to 1982, and that is when I met Susan. She rented a small share of the space on the second floor, and so we were studio mates for at least a year. I was painting large expressionistic paintings on canvas at that time. When we married in 1982 and realized that we had Dylan and Jen to support, we began to create ways of working together, primarily by working on public art projects like murals, doing gallery installations, painting banners, and working in schools as visiting artists. Many of the projects we took on had fiber or fabric as a part of their design. Gradually, because of Susan's background in quilt making and the huge revival of interest in quilt making in the last twenty years, we began to blend our skills into the making of folk art quilts.

"My role is usually to do the pattern, one generated from an idea we've had and talked about executing. I do the drawing, the cutting, the silk screening of images and alphabet letters if we are going to use a quote. Susan then does the sewing, making decisions as she goes. If she gets stuck, then we huddle and figure it out together. Some of the quilts resemble me—have my aesthetic—and some reveal more of Susan's aesthetic, but much of the overall design work is the result of collaboration. We consider it a luxury to have one another. I don't sew and Susan doesn't draw, at least conceptually. So our areas of expertise overlap really well."

"Actually, I do draw," Susan adds, "but I work from life. I generally get the reference materials together for the concept and then work with Mark on the composition. Mark draws directly out of his head. He is amazingly good at imagining something and then drawing it.

"The design is roughed out on paper, first as a sketch and later to scale. Our ideas come from many places: from things we have read, poetry, places we've visited, the natural world, even dreams. Then I work

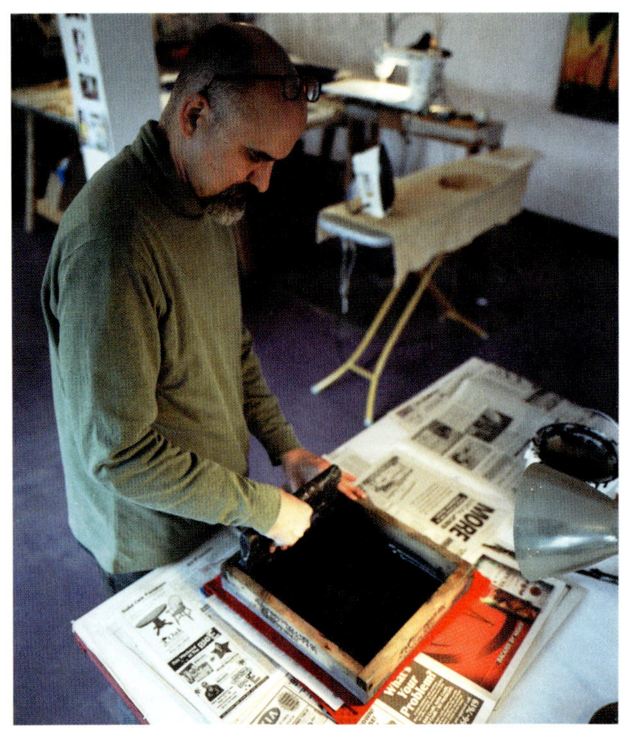

Mark, with silk-screening equipment

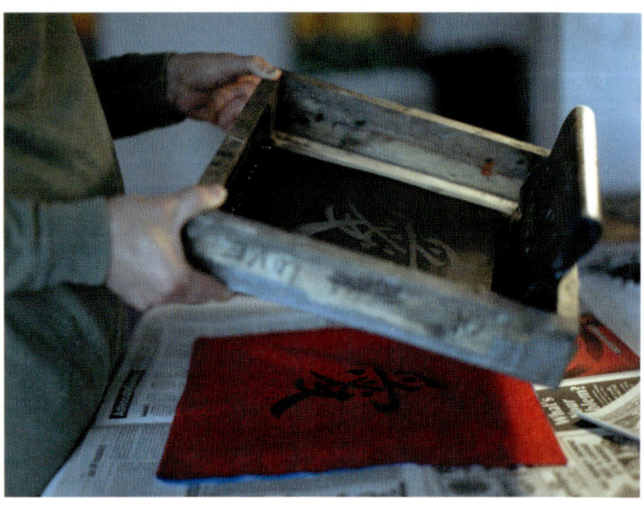

Mark: "I do the drawing, the cutting, the silk screening of images and alphabet letters."

directly on a piece of 100 percent cotton batting. Once the pattern is traced onto the batting, I will sew the fabric directly onto it. That's one way our method of making quilts differs from the traditional way— where you have three layers: a front, constructed completely, a layer of batting, and a back which is either brought around to overlap the front or is bound at the edge. By sewing directly on the batting and by working from the middle rather than from the edges, each design I make is constructed as I go along, piece by piece, always building, always responding to what came before and what needs to follow. I think it's that organic growth that creates the most distinctive and original component of our work. That each piece is a different size, perhaps a different color, gives the work an improvisional quality; it has room to go a variety of ways. That room for opportunity is very exciting.

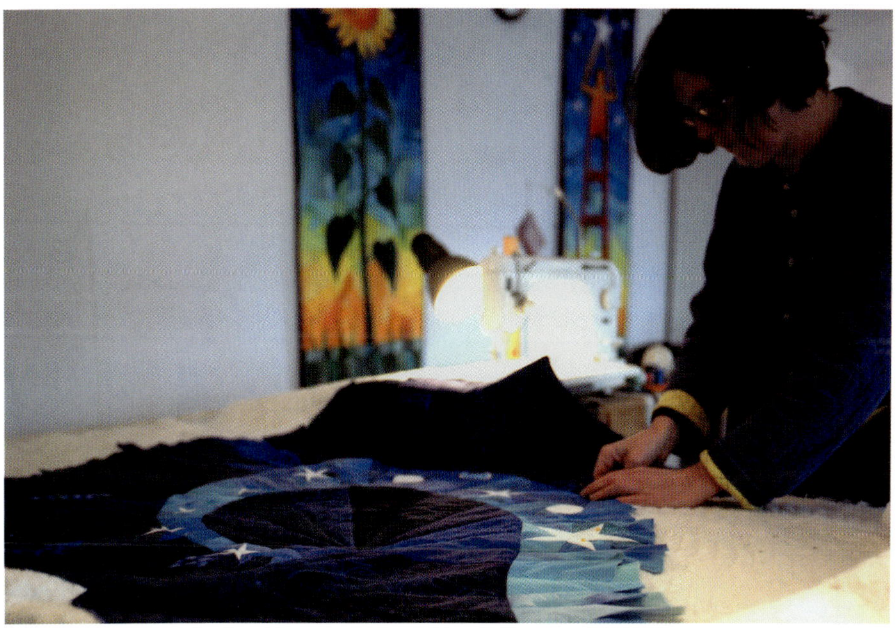

Susan: "I work from the center, organically outward."

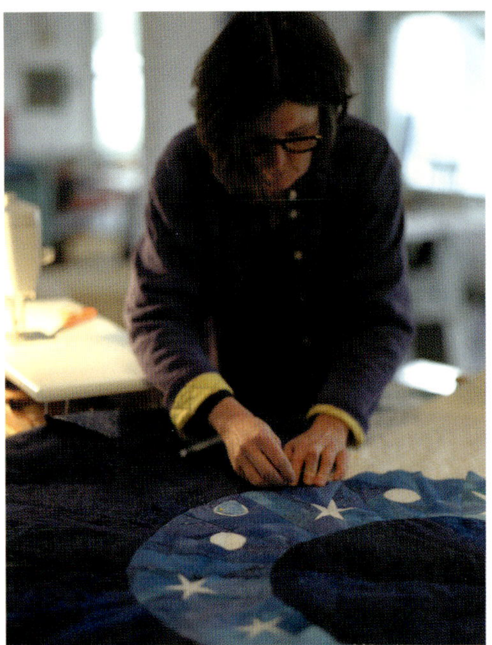

Susan, pinning and sewing by hand directly on the cotton batting

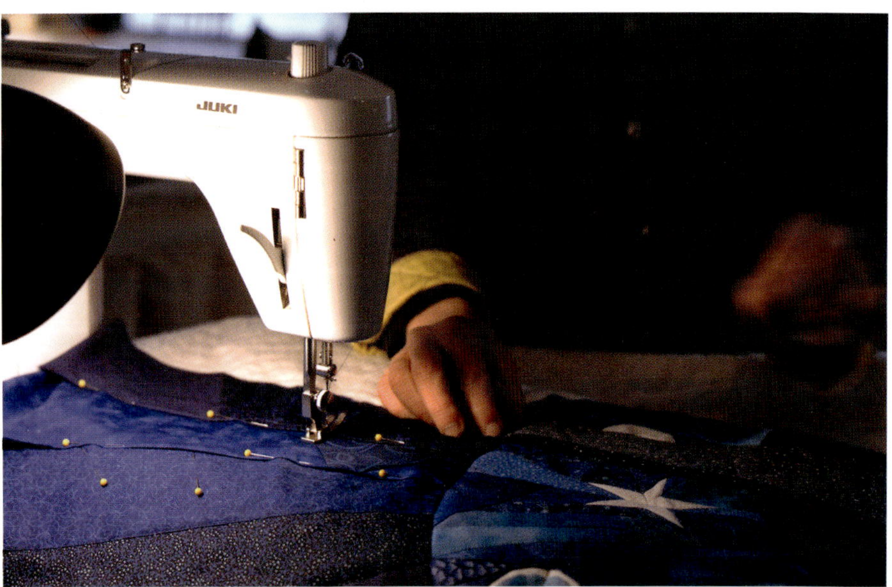

Susan also machine-stitches directly onto the batting. "Each piece is a different size, perhaps a different color, so it gives the work an improvisational quality."

"Of course, that's not to say that we haven't been influenced by many traditions in quilting. Amish quilts, with their strong geometric designs and use of black, attract me. And Victorian crazy quilts, that 'parlor craft' practiced by groups of nineteenth-century women who saved valuable pieces of velvet and silk which they pieced onto muslin squares, then sewed into quilts, intrigue me. They are highly ornate, often embroidered on top of the quilting with beautiful stitching like 'turkey tracks' or 'French knots'—in short, showcases for the women's talent. But I think one quilt tradition that delivered a real wallop occurred when we went to see an exhibit of African American 'strip quilts' at Williams College. You can sense the African sensibility in how design is used, how the quilts are woven in strips, mimicking the way cloth was made in Africa, and in their absolutely fearless use of color. Often they're not rectilinear or perfect in symmetry of design. But they are all about motion and color and energy and the execution of an idea. They break all the 'rules,' and from them I resolved to use tradition when it worked for me and to invent my own solutions when it didn't."

Mark goes over to turn up the heater. The studio dog, Sandy, moves even closer to the warmth. Mark and Susan are wearing fleece vests and, like Sandy, seem to know the value of sitting close to the heater on this raw March morning.

"Studying painting has also been a strong influence on us," Mark adds slowly, "particularly the work of Kandinsky, Miro, Van Gogh, and especially Paul Klee. We go to museums whenever we travel in Europe and the United States and look at functional art as well as fine art. It is, after all, the underlying geometry that really powers our work, not embellishments. Our designs have lots of action, but they also display a level of simplicity and clarity. We collect fabric and buy it wherever we go, liking to use both vintage and new materials.

"We try to be open to old traditions in quilting, for example, creating a quilt to commemorate an occasion, either private or public. We created

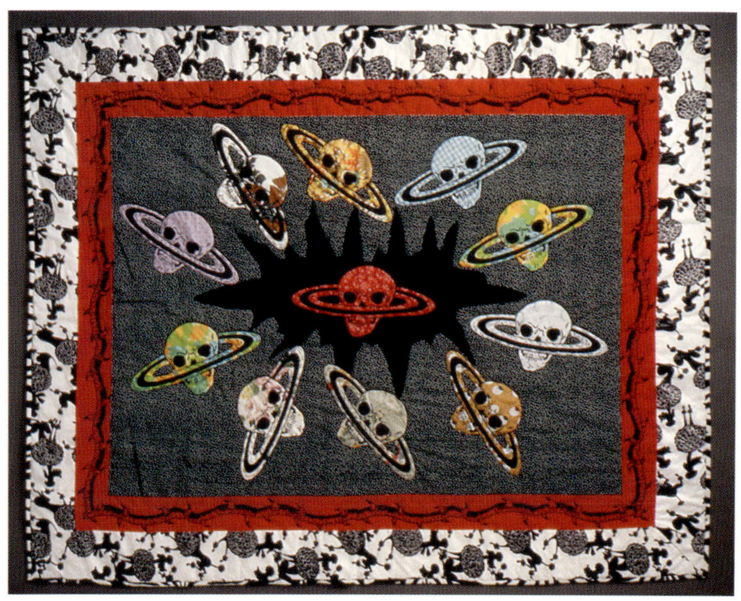

Susan and Mark's completed quilts. "We like to mix the traditional with the innovative, contributing something fresh to a tradition we honor."

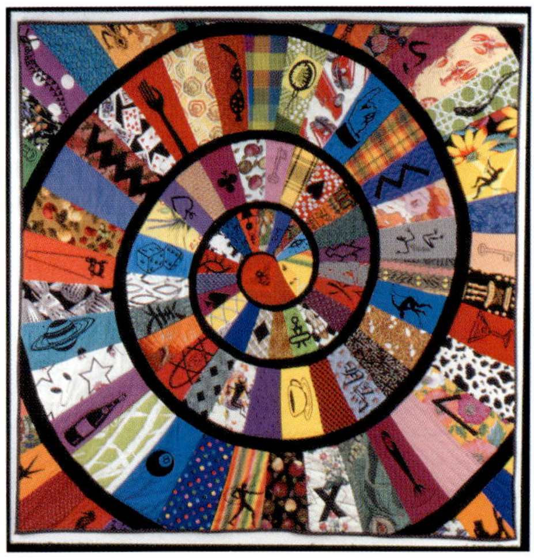

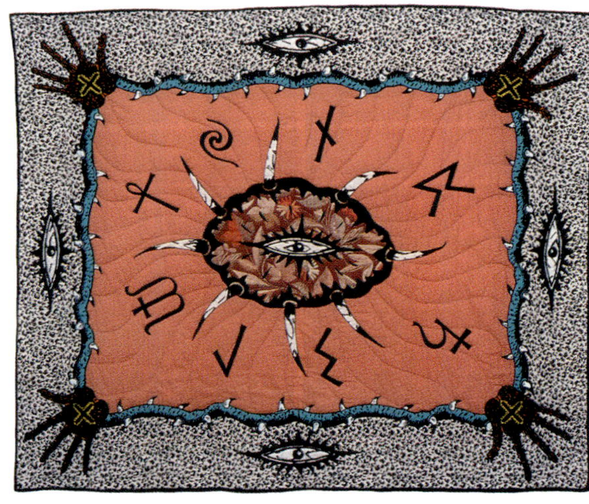

a 'threshold' pattern for a quilt commemorating the millennium in much the same way that a nineteenth-century quilter might have created a Civil War quilt. Or we employ symbols like the open hand, the tree of life, a flower, a bird, that have appeared in utilitarian bed quilts for hundreds of years. But we also bring our unique vision to our quilts, and in that way we're not simply inheriting a tradition but contributing to its ongoing evolution."

Susan nods her agreement. "There is an exciting creative tension in Mark's and my collaboration." Mark smiles. "And, of course, quilting is, historically, a collaborative art. We realize every day that we are indebted to the thousands of anonymous quilters whose work we have enjoyed and whose efforts have informed our own process. We add our contributions to that ever-changing, ever-growing tradition."

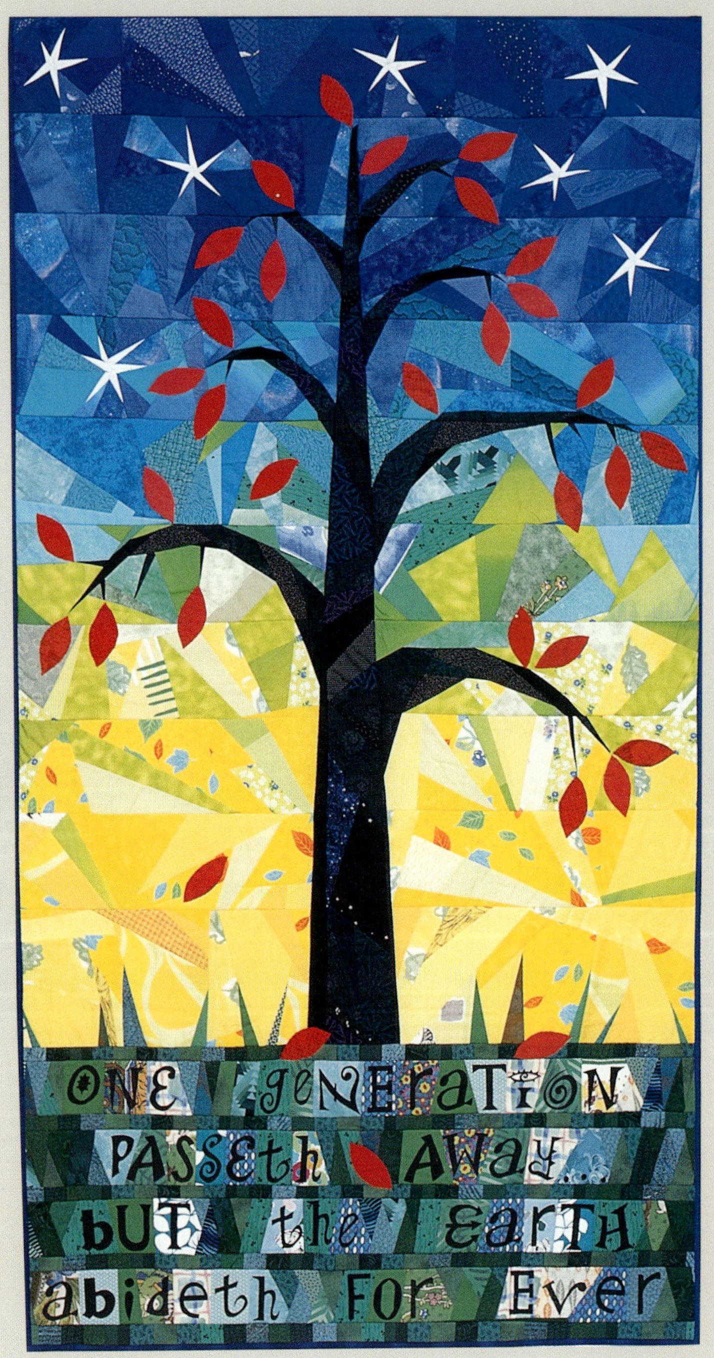

ONE GENERATION
PASSETH AWAY...
bUT the EARTH
abideth FOR Ever

"ONE GENERATION PASSETH AWAY. . . BUT THE EARTH ABIDETH FOREVER"

90" × 48"

"MARK AND I conceived the idea for this quilt while driving across the Midwest on our return from San Francisco. Although we had made a symbolic quilt, 'Garden of Eden,' and a full cut, silk-screened, printed and painted pictorial quilt, 'Fruit of the Tree,' we still felt there was much more to explore in the "creation story" and its attendant symbols and images. When we got back home, Mark sketched a rough cartoon of the tree, which hung on the wall of the studio for a year.

"I had been making a series of spiral quilts that began in the center and built outward on a base of cotton batting. Each piece was stitched, then topstitched to create an ever-widening curvilinear sweep of color and fabric. I determined that I would keep the improvisional aspect of that process, but would begin the piece at the horizon line and work upwards, piecing in the limbs and branches of the tree within the context of the background. The horizon was to be bright, as if it was dawn or dusk, and I planned to crown the top of the piece with stars.

"I began with the richest, most vibrant shades of yellow, gradually building both sides of the field color simultaneously in panels. I realized that I was going to have to move the color gradation along if I was to reach deep blue at the top of the quilt. Then that mysterious rhythm began, the one that, in the best of circumstances, carries the work and you along with it. The top panel of deep blue had an asymmetrical crown of stars. On impulse, I cut about twenty red leaf-shaped pieces and laid them on the quilt. Mark came in to look and he just said, 'Yes.'

"Mark had designed an alphabet using various fonts and we began to search for our text. Since the tree had evolved into a symbol of life, of shelter, of growth, we chose a quote from Ecclesiastes, "One generation passeth away . . . but the earth abideth forever."

—Susan Boss

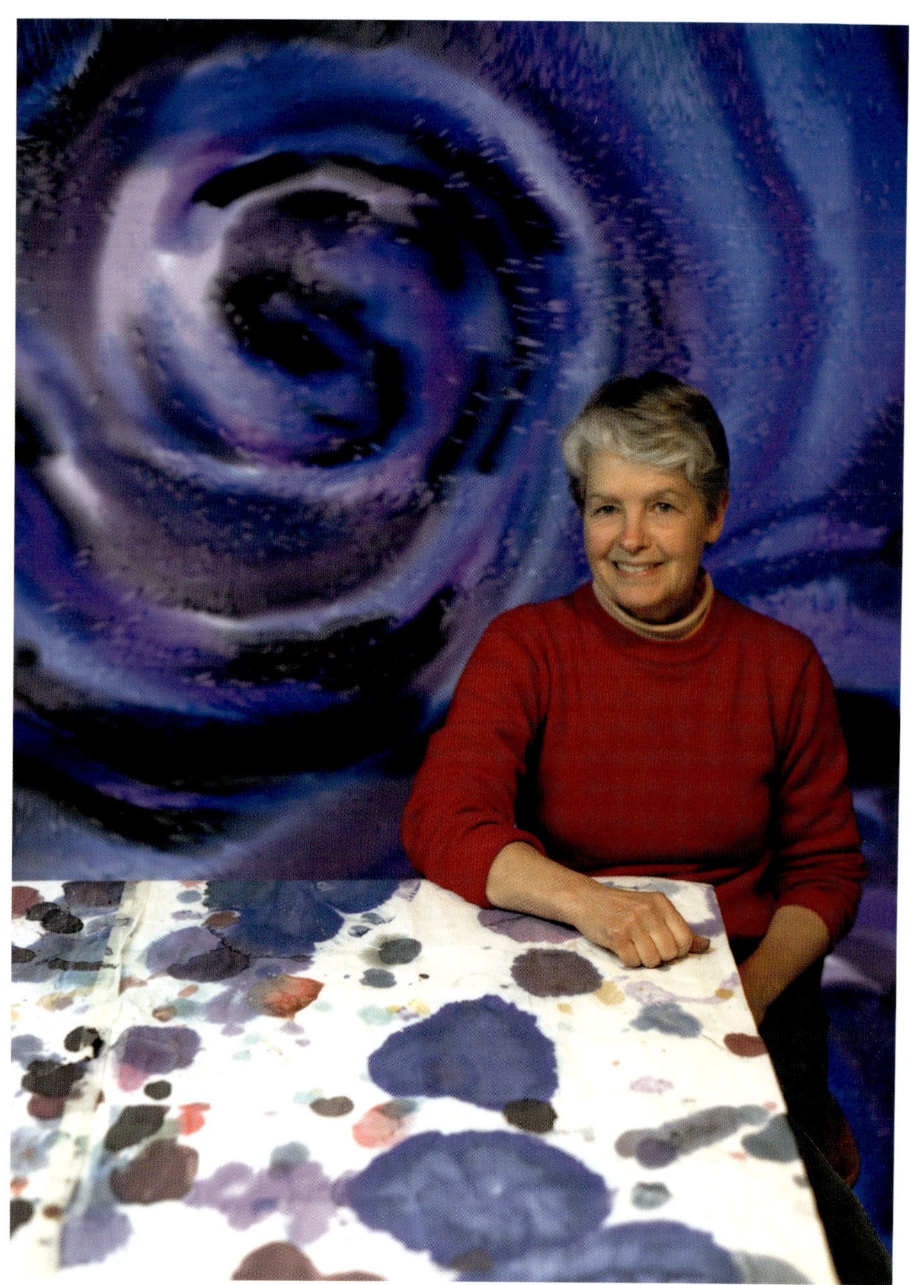

Sally Dillon

SALLY DILLON

Hand-painted Wearable Art, Silk Quilts

SALLY DILLON's home, just a few miles east of Amherst, is alive with beautifully dyed and painted silk wall hangings, bed quilts, place mats, and handmade furniture. Reminders of her artistic heritage also line the walls: A mountain range collage executed by her artist mother and a rhythmic grouping of antique tools, part of a large collection of hand tools collected and used by her late father, a woodworker, are the focal points of the dining room and den, respectively. Sally's studio is in the basement of the home, a large multistationed work space that contains a number of washbasins and tubs as well as rows of large flat-topped worktables. She stretches the highest-quality white silk over frames, then draws a resist line with wax before applying French dyes with soft watercolor brushes. The silk is then dried, steamed, washed, and dry-cleaned before being assembled into quilts or wearable art. Rows of silk scarves at various stages of completion hang on one side of the room, while breathtakingly beautiful lined silk jackets hang in another corner, away from any direct light.

Upstairs again, Sally unfolds several completed quilts, explaining their origins and a bit of their execution as she smooths them out on a table or chair. She is petite, with hands that look almost too small to do all she asks of them. But her energy fills the room, even as she hushes Chester, the black Lab who insists on joining the conversation.

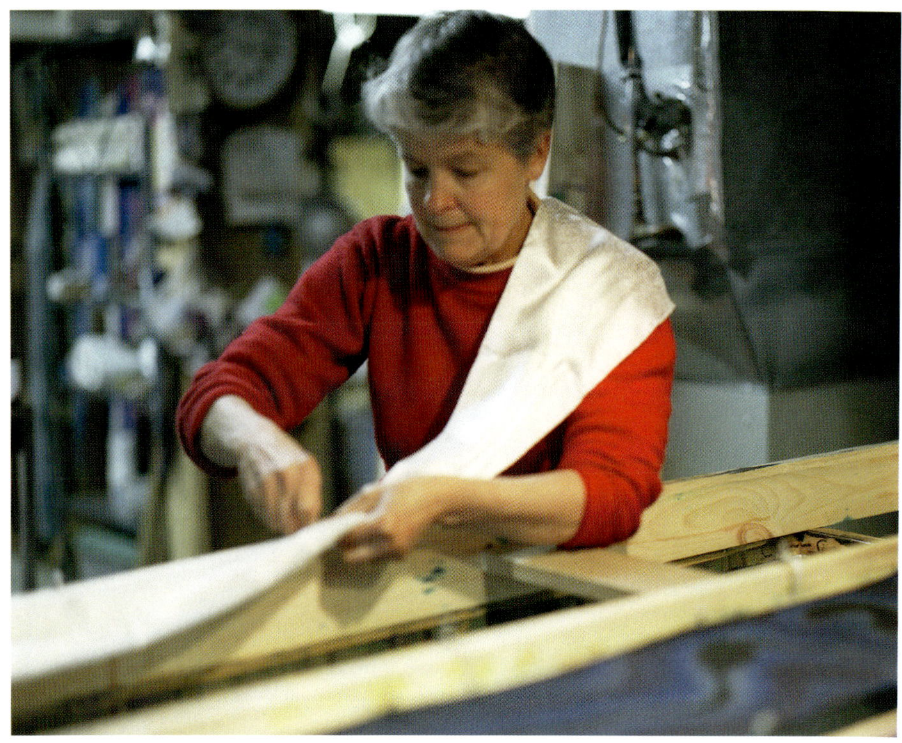

Stretching high-quality silk, pinning it on wooden frames

"This piece is called the 'Massachusetts Quilt,' or sometimes 'Thoughts of Home.' I painted it when I was living in Texas, hoping to move back to Massachusetts. The coastline moves from Boston Harbor to the Elizabeth Islands, the most recognizable parts of Massachusetts from the air. This whale identifies the edge of the continental shelf. And the small panels depict the hills of Fitchburg, my hometown; a trout, my father's favorite fish; and Hurricane Bob—which we experienced firsthand."

She unfolds a second quilt, one that also employs predominantly the deep royal blues of the previous quilt, but adds oranges and burnt

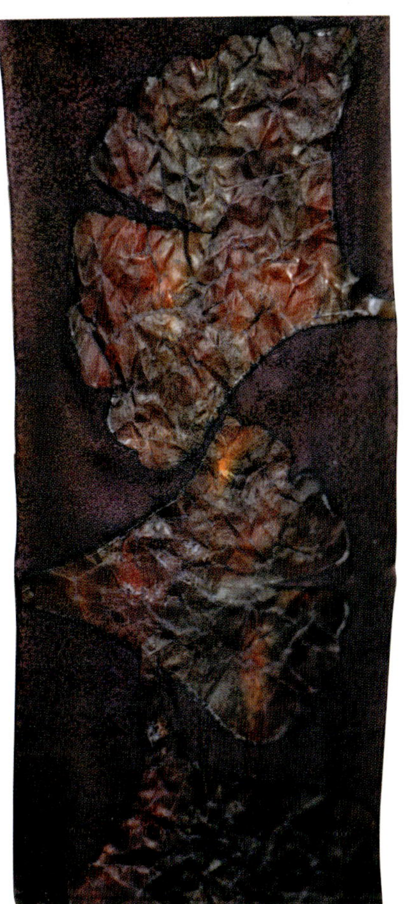

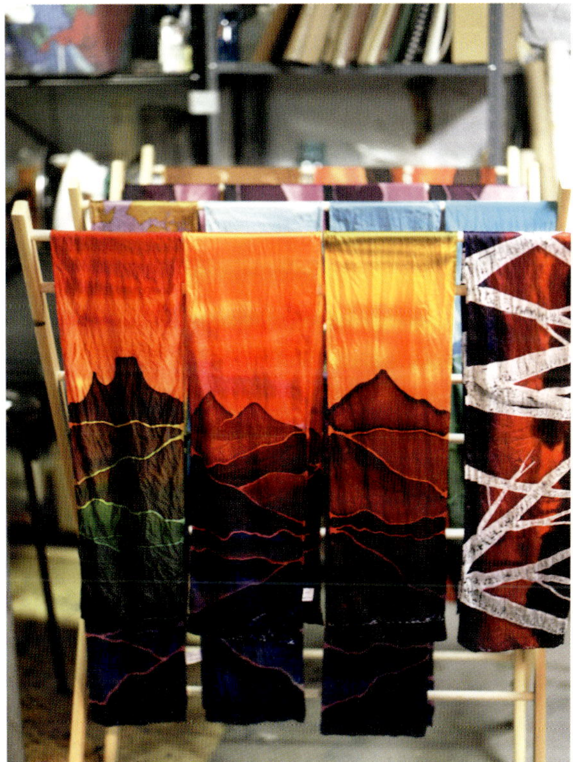

Rows of drying silk scarves. Subsequently, they will be steamed, washed, and dry-cleaned.

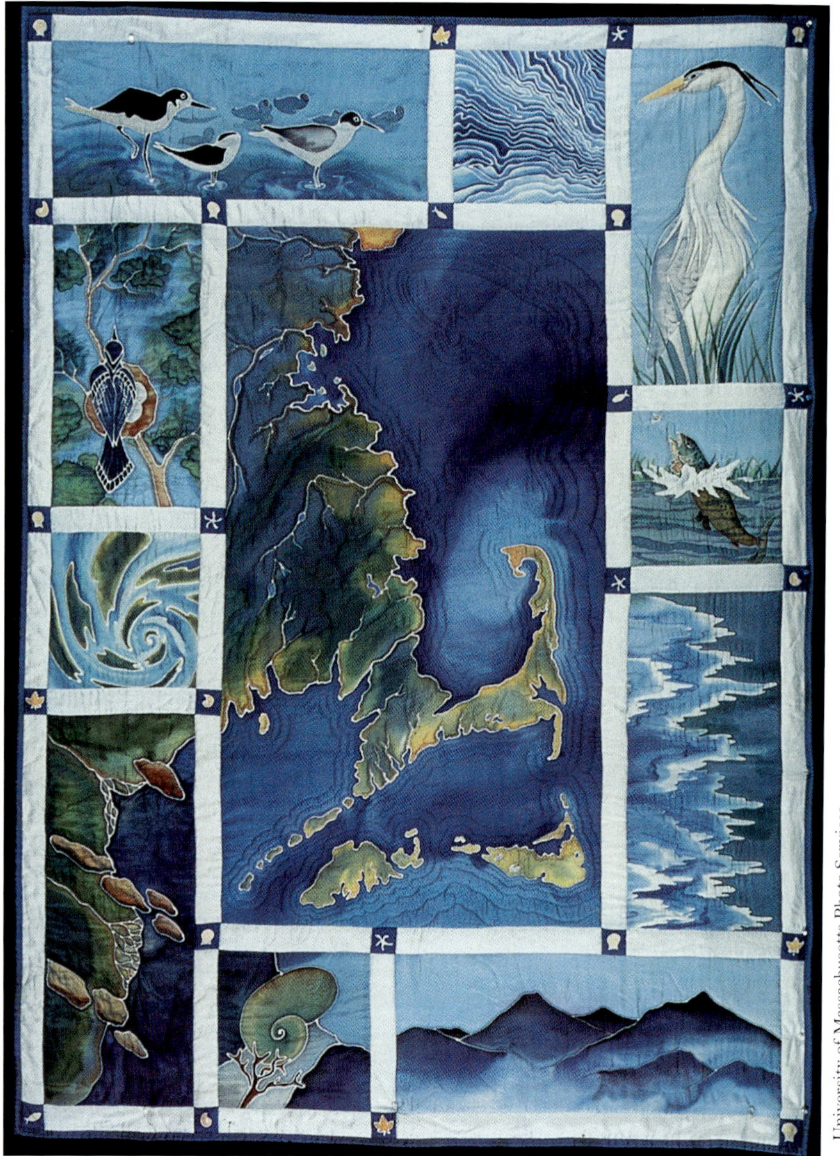

"Thoughts of Home," in memory of Jay Allan Hall, 80" × 63"; hand-quilted by Ruth Anderson, Dallas, Texas. Sally painted the quilt while living in Texas and hoping to return to Massachusetts.

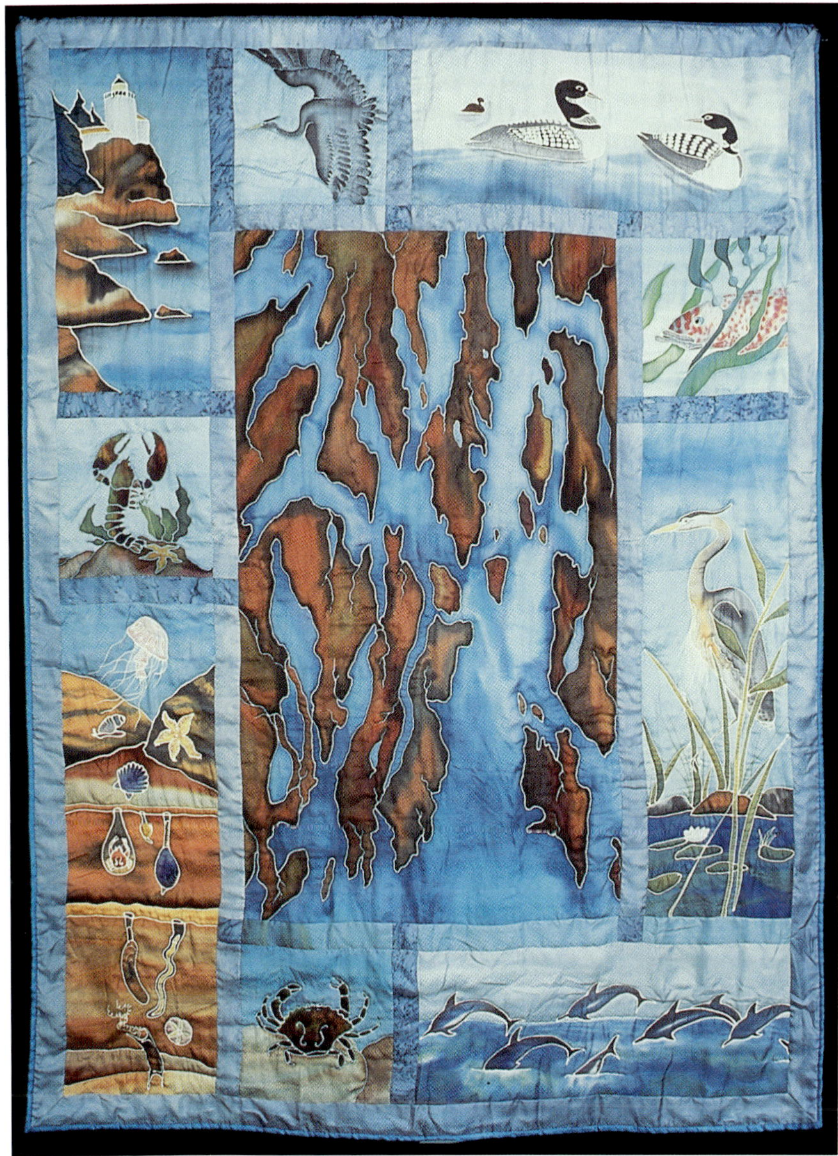

"Coast of Maine," 83″ × 63″, *hand-quilted by Sally Weymouth of Bailey Island, Maine. This quilt map includes some of Sally Dillon's favorite spots: Westport Island and the Sheepscot River near Boothbay Harbor.*

sienna to its panels. "This is called 'The Coast of Maine' and depicts on its map the areas of Boothbay Harbor, Wiscasset, and Westport Island. The smaller panels are of a lighthouse, herons, loons, and dolphins, as well as fish, lobster, and crabs that are well below the waterline."

In addition to the accurate topography and aerial mapping evident on both quilts, intricate borders—sashing, as it's called—"frame" each of the panels. Expert stitching and quilting enhance the designs even further, creating patterns on the cloth, veins on the leaves, delineation in the flora and fauna. These "frames within a frame" combine to tell a story, sometimes by linking quite literal objects and, at other times, by using the power of suggestion—the juxtaposition of different perspectives, different angles of vision, different ways of experiencing one geographic region. Sally's quilts make one *see* and *feel* simultaneously—a region, a season, an underwater world, a mountaintop view.

"Both my husband and I grew up in Fitchburg; both sides of my family have lived in New England since the 1600s. I loved being surrounded by natural beauty, the kind of New England beauty that possesses intimate scale and close proximity to walkable mountain trails and forest preserves and rivers, and of course, Maine and the ocean. We went often to the seashore when I was growing up, and I think much of my love for watery regions came from spending time there, exploring, collecting shells, looking at little sea creatures.

When it was time for college I went to Mount Holyoke College, where I loved that landscape too—ringed with mountains, cut by the broad Connecticut River. I went with the intention of studying chemistry, but after I took an art course from Leonard DeLonga, I knew I had found my life's work. I graduated with a B.A. in art, and then traveled west to an entirely new landscape, where I took an M.A. in art from the University of New Mexico. When my soon-to-be-husband got a job at Southern Methodist University in Dallas, we decided to marry and move to Dallas. We never intended to stay. But it was an exciting place to be in the early seventies: lots of energy for creative projects, lots of money for people in the arts. I landed a terrific job with a commercial art company. I designed and installed big sculptures for malls, made banners, kinetic sculptures for public spaces, I welded things, I designed theater backdrops and made set designs and stage paintings. For a time, with my husband's teaching job and my job as art director for this exciting company, we thought we were living a fabulous life—especially for two who had never, up to a few years before, been west of the Hudson River.

"Then we decided to adopt children. And our notions of 'just experimenting' in Dallas converted into a much longer range 'settling in.' We really had to stay put, since both of us had good jobs, and when babies arrive on the scene, moving becomes much less attractive. Actually, when our son arrived in our lives, I had just enrolled in a scuba-diving class. We had been told by the adoption agency that our wait for a baby would be a long one—'sometimes it takes years,' that sort of thing— so I had signed up to learn to dive, to learn to explore the fascinating sea in a more intimate way. Suddenly, our son arrived. Just two weeks old and all of five pounds. I can remember going off to my scuba class and literally calling my husband every fifteen minutes or so, saying things like, 'Is he eating anything?,' or 'Is he still breathing?' Without the nine months' preparation time, suddenly parenting a child is a shock, even if a wonderful shock. And suddenly, the fabulous job didn't seem so fabulous anymore. Often I had to work on weekends to install things, or be gone in the evenings when I was wanted and needed at home.

"So I began to think through the things I did in the arts that I both loved and that would also mesh with having babies around. (For after we had our first baby, we thought, *This is so much fun. Let's do it again.* Our daughter arrived several years later.) Welding now didn't seem so practical. And I didn't want anything too toxic around the house, or

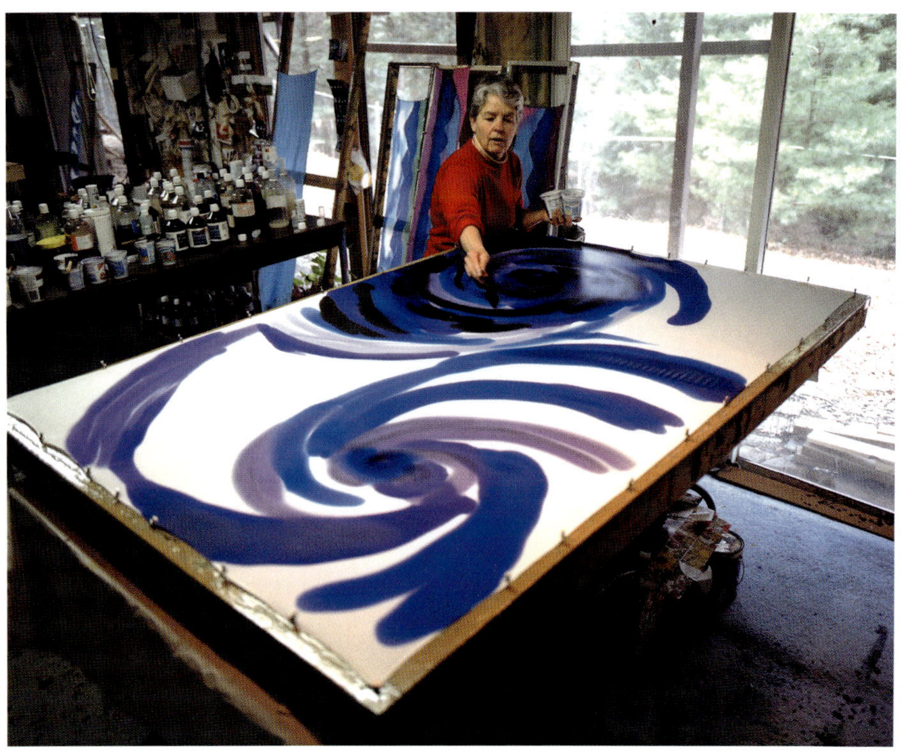

"Silk and dye make magic."

anything that required me to be all suited-up. Painting, particularly painting on silk, is a good 'stop and start' process. You don't have to have long uninterrupted periods of time. And besides, I love silk—its texture, flow, and the way it takes the dye. Silk and dye make magic.

"Painting on silk also allowed me to explore another interest: geology. My first silk paintings were of rocks, minerals, and rock formations. I designed them to be framed and hung on a wall. I had a big show of structural geology paintings in Hannover, Germany. I did a series of geological paintings that were shown at the Harvard Mineralogical and Geological Museum. That led to an interest in

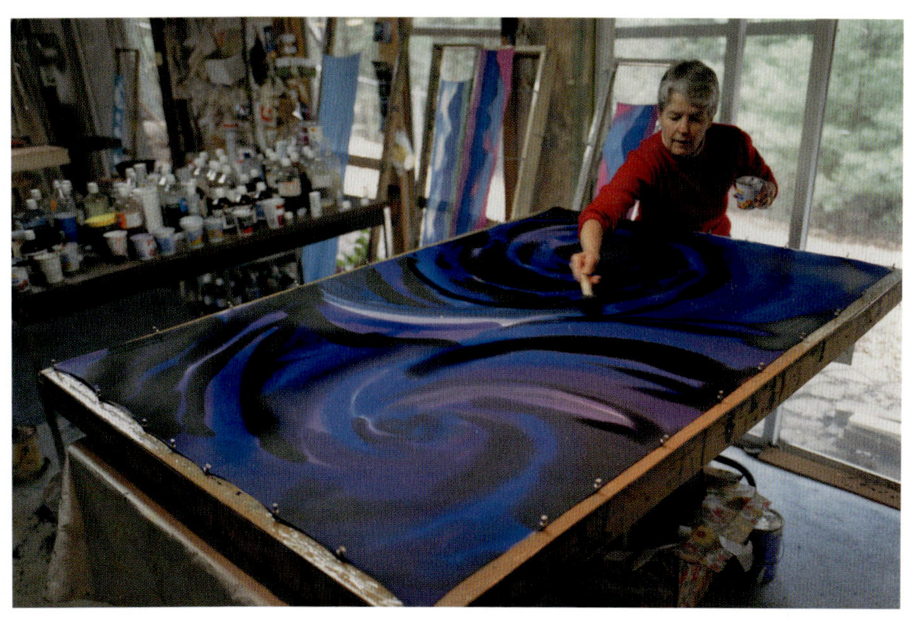

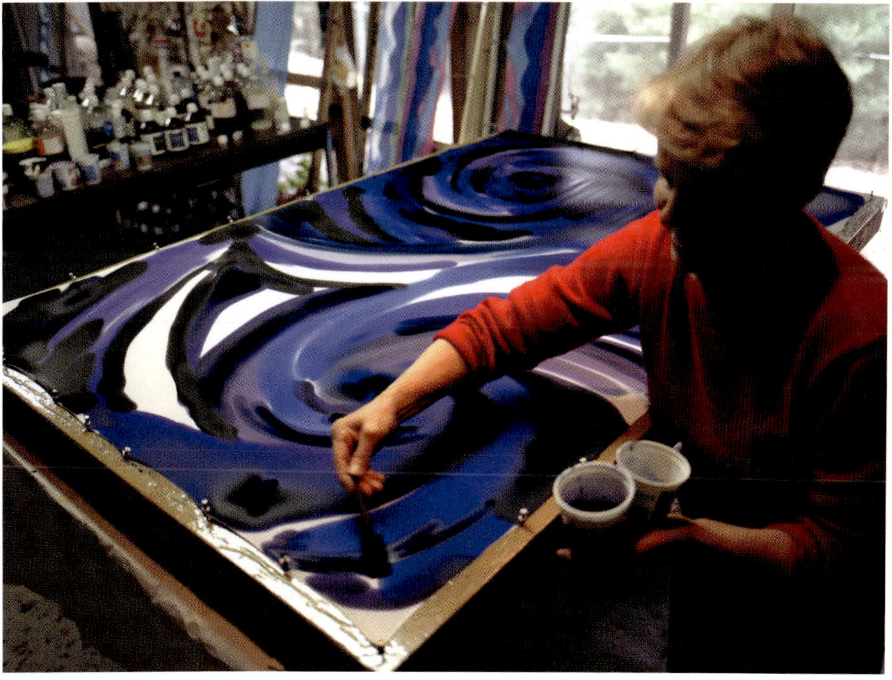

mapping—topographical, cross-sectional maps—and aerial photography. I gradually started adding indigenous animals and birds to panels.

"I moved from the solid framed wall hangings to supple quilts as a consequence of a misunderstanding. A Boston architect had asked me to make a very large framed wall hanging for him (he had described the space), which I executed while still in Texas, wrapped and shipped the whole thing—which weighed several hundred pounds—to my father in Massachusetts. We uncrated it together and took it to the architectural location to hang it. The architect had failed to mention that the space was actually in a stairwell. So my father and I had to go out and buy wood to construct a scaffolding in order to get the thing hung. I thought to myself as we were hefting this giant around, why not produce something soft, lightweight, something that 'floats'—a quilt. And I think I also saw then, just as I see now, some intrinsic value in making functional things: quilts to hang as well as quilts to keep you warm, or jackets and scarves that can make the wearer feel special. Moving from purely presentational art to wearable and functional art satisfies that part of me that wants to make something usable. Is that a Yankee thing, do you think?"

We laugh together at the obvious accuracy of this remark. As Sally pours tea, I ask about the traditions that inform her art.

"My quilts are part of a larger tradition in quilting: story quilts, or narrative quilts. The American Folk Art Museum in New York has many fine examples of story quilts. There are examples from the 1800s where a whole community, or at least the women in the community, would gather together to develop a quilt which told the history of the community: Churches would be pictured, probably the town hall, perhaps pictures of the founding fathers, important buildings or landmarks. This type of quilt was usually hung in a public space, perhaps the court house or the town hall. On smaller scale but in the same narrative vein, story quilts were also created to preserve the history of a family, its settlement in a particular area, ancestors, births, deaths. It was meant to be an historic document, a permanent record and celebration of the past.

"But there are also wonderful contemporary story quilts. Faith Ringgold, for example, the African American contemporary quilter, has created a whole series of remarkable quilts representing her life as she was growing up in New York City. One of her quilts has become the illustrative text of a children's book titled *Tar Beach*, for it tells the story of children going to their 'beach,' the rooftops of high-rise apartment buildings, to play, to picnic, to gaze at the stars on hot summer nights. There is a worldwide tradition of storytelling quilts in a variety of cultures. I like to think that I'm a part of it.

"When our children were old enough to be easily mobile, my husband and I thought more and more about returning to New England. We wanted them to have some of the same opportunities we had grown up with—exploring forests and rivers, and lakes and the ocean, rather than the intensely urban environment of Dallas. We've been back in New England for eight years, and it really has felt like coming home. I'm delighted to have the Fiber Art Center newly opened in Amherst, a place where exhibits can be hung, and classes and workshops in all forms of fiber art can be given. The nature of the work is, as with all arts, fairly solitary. And having the center is like having a focal point, a meeting place for artists who are of a similar mind.

"Gradually I learned that I don't have to do every single facet of the work myself. When I started, I designed everything, dyed, painted, sewed, assembled, installed, kept the books, everything. But I've come to see that I don't do all things equally well. I sew less well than I paint, for example. So when I create a one-of-a-kind silk jacket that a woman is asked to pay a lot of money to own, I hire an expert seamstress to ensure that the stitching and the proportions are exactly right. Or when I want a piece of exquisite hand-quilting, I turn to Janet Hale in nearby

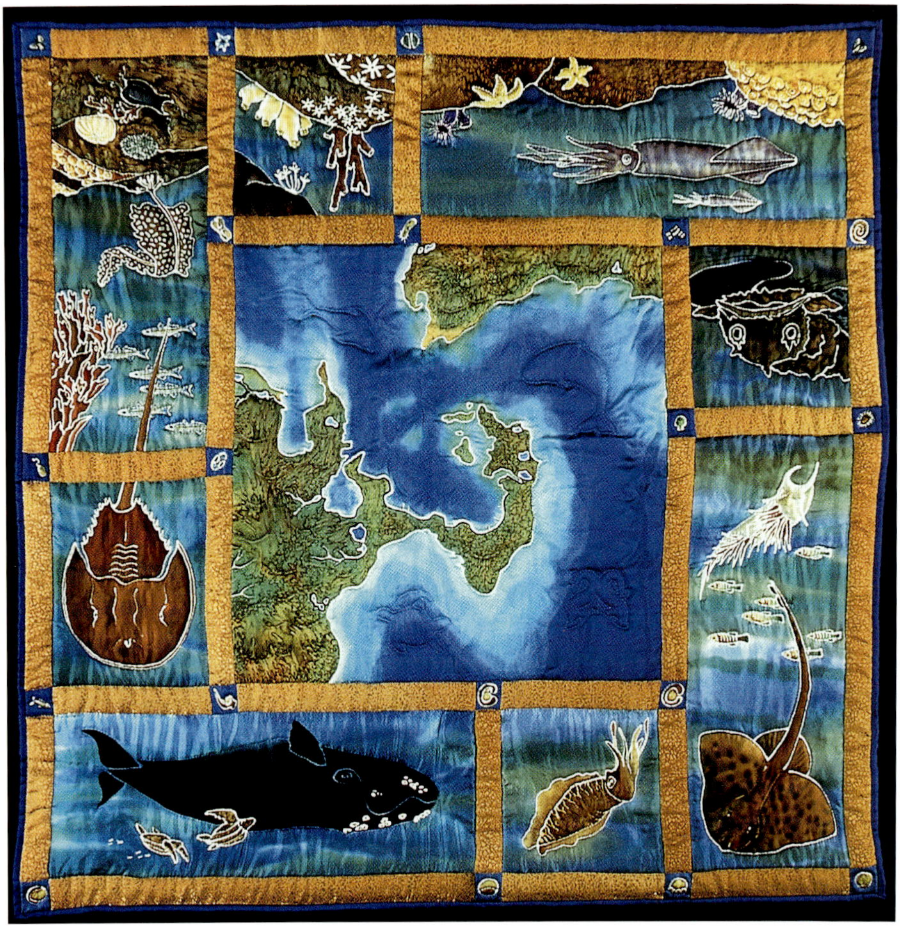

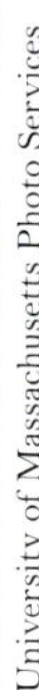

"Woods Hole," 48" × 48", hand-quilted by Janet Hale of Whately, Massachusetts. The center map is of the Woods Hole area on Cape Cod, Massachusetts, home of the Marine Biological Laboratory.

Whately, who is superbly skilled in hand-quilting. I've learned that it's much better to let go of some of the controls—that, in fact, certain kinds of collaboration produce an even better piece of work."

I asked Sally whether most of her work is commissioned, or whether she creates quilts on subjects that simply appeal to her.

"The past two years have been more or less consumed by several major commissions. The first was a quilt commemorating and depicting the silk industry that blossomed in Northampton in the 1830s. Northampton's silk industry is a fascinating story, and Marjorie Senechal, a professor at Smith College, along with Historic Northampton's museum director, decided to put together an exhibit and a symposium telling some of its highlights. Many of the colonies experimented with raising silkworms, but it was in the Connecticut River Valley where the mulberry trees thrived and where the first mills were established. Until it all unraveled in the 1930s with changing fashions and the development of synthetic cloth, it was home to not only the manufacture of silk, but also to the Corticelli Silk Company, which became one of the largest manufacturers of thread in the world. I loved researching and learning about this story as I planned the quilt.

"At the same time I was commissioned to do a Woods Hole quilt for a researcher at the Marine Biological Laboratory at Woods Hole, Massachusetts. It, in a scientific way, has its own fascinations since each of the little sea creatures pictured on the quilt is used for important medical and scientific research. For example, scientists draw blood from the horseshoe crabs, like these pictured in the quilt, and use it to test for any bacteria in insulin supplies. Each of these sea creatures has to be scientifically accurate—drawn to the last detail, the last hair.

"I love commission work—and am grateful for it. But it has claimed much of my life of late. I think it's time to look around and spot something *I* want to do—just for me, out of my imagination. That won't be hard. The concept and early stages of design always excite me. And then there's that application of the dye to the silk, when anything can happen."

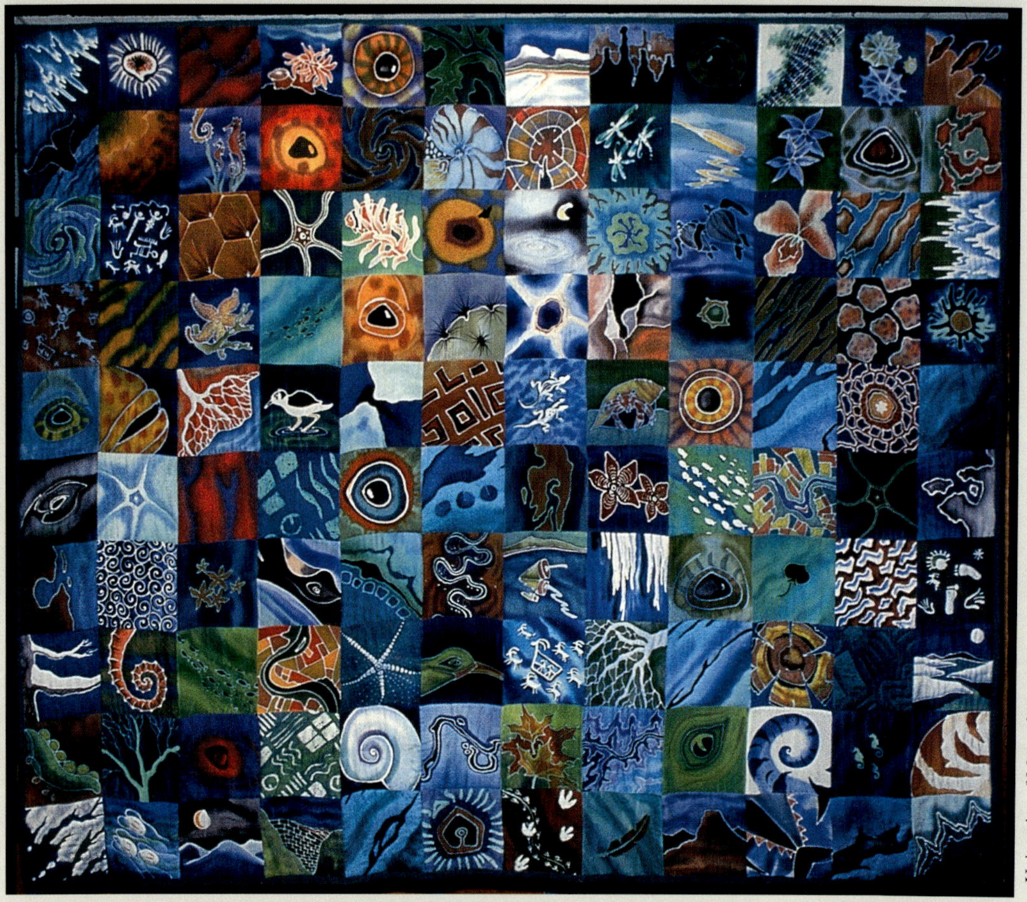

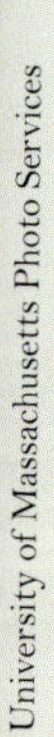
University of Massachusetts Photo Services

MEMORY QUILT

91" × 108"
Hand-quilting by Sally Weymouth,
Bailey Island, Maine

"I MADE THIS QUILT as a twenty-fifth anniversary present for my husband. Each of the 120 squares depicts a favorite memory. Poring over old photos, postcards, and letters to find just the right images was a great joy. Included are favorite places we have shared, such as the Coast of Maine, Bryce Canyon, Big Bend, and the Colorado River. Some panels represent a special moment, such as the lunar eclipse reflected in a tide pool in Maine and camping with the tortoises in the Galapagos Islands.

"My intention was to find just the right images that would reflect twenty-five years' worth of small moments, sewn together to make a marriage. That may sound a little sentimental, but in our case, it really is true. The biggest challenge was not making it twice as big. I actually had lots of additional squares that did not make the cut. Although they represented good memories, they were just not quite the right shape or color to fit into the design. Usually I make a very detailed pattern for a quilt, but in this case I made all the squares over a long period of time, then determined the layout by the shape of their configurations and by their colors. They are not arranged chronologically or grouped by subject, but rather have a fluidity directed only by overall design and moving color."

—Sally Dillon

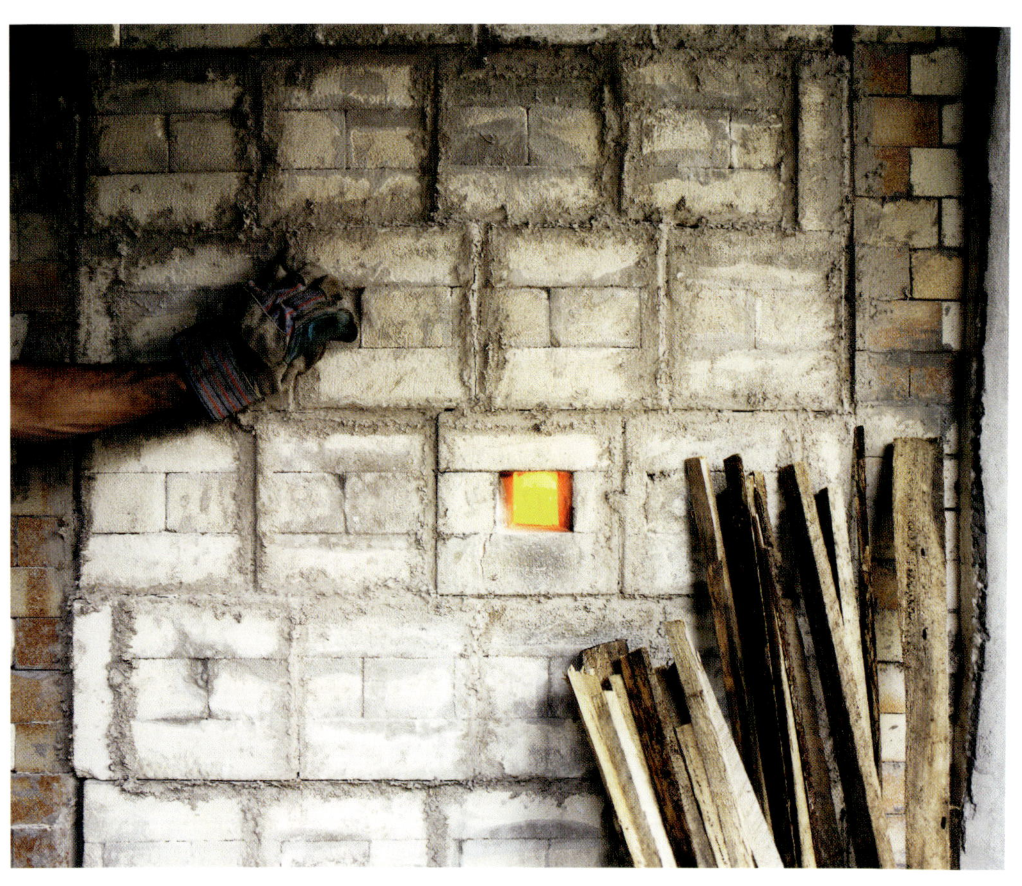

A TOUCH OF GRACE

I T IS A NEW ENGLAND autumn morning. Despite yesterday's torren-
tial rains, which open huge wading pools in the parking lots of the
Northampton Fairgrounds, a queue of perhaps fifty people wait eagerly
for the gates to open on the Paradise City Arts Festival. This juried festival, founded by local artists Linda and Geoffrey Post, draws approximately ten thousand visitors each spring and fall. More than three
hundred artists working in media ranging from glass to ceramics,
sculpture to fiber arts, are housed in individual booths sheltered within
the fairgounds' pavilions. Not only are the artists there to display and
sell their work, they also pride themselves on conversing with visitors,
often explaining in detail a particular technique or process important
to their craft. I know chances are good that I'll see Sally, Josh, Walter,
Susan, and Mark at Paradise City, but also a host of new artists, some
from California, Oregon, Florida, and South Carolina, all talking ani-
matedly to a rapt audience. What accounts for the extraordinary success of such an enterprise? What draws people from all walks of life to
the alchemy of the creative process? What creates the hunger to see
and touch the objects of its inspiration?

I suspect a deep and abiding aesthetic response lies within us all.
We savor the effort, admire the shapeliness, the color, the pattern, the
patina of something unique and perfectly made. And the admiration we
feel for what is perfectly made extends to its maker. The process of
translating a mental image into an engraving, a vase, a quilt, a jar, a
bowl excites the imagination, offers some of the same "surprise and

delight" that Robert Frost suggests are the trademarks of the good poem.

Aesthetic appreciation also connects us to the traditions that gather in all their cumulative power under and around the individual artists. To touch a Mark Shapiro jar or a Josh Simpson cup is to feel not only the work of the last few centuries, but also the longer exploratory reach back into the cultures of indigenous peoples, their artifacts, the records of their history. Art's timelessness rescues us from immersion in the contemporary. We are invited to participate in something larger than ourselves, longer than "now."

As I visited in the homes and studios of the artists, collecting the interviews for this book, I was drawn, both consciously and unconsciously, into closer proximity to their artistic process. If the creative process remains a deeply mysterious and idiosyncratic experience, I came to understand much more fully how artists describe the work that they do, how they see their own relationship to it. I discovered that while I could not invent some invisible template that guided the cut of their creativity (they resisted all easy generalizations), I could discover common denominators in their personal stories. When viewed collectively, a pattern of parallel journeys emerged.

For example, all are superbly creative problem solvers and their solutions are powerfully visual. Tai Hazard's glimpse of the curve in the prow of a Viking ship thirty years ago finds its replication in the graceful curves of her furniture. Carol Blinn's exquisite use of color, sometimes creating mood, sometimes evoking a cultural epoch, wells up from a kind of Jungian unconscious; "I even dream in color," she confesses. When Barry Moser confides, "I see the holy in the commonplace. I see its footprints everywhere. . . ," the rationale for a truck driver becoming Hezekiah and a cook becoming Jesus becomes clear. Seeing something others do not see is the mark of any visionary. Being able to transmute that special vision into something tangible, dimensional, functional, beautiful is the mark of the artist.

I was surprised to learn that a number of the artists are self-taught. Yet each alludes to the influence and significance of some kind of mentor. In some instances it is a specific teacher or benefactor like Harold McGrath or Karen Karnes. Susan Boss, Mark Brown, Ken Salem, Sally Dillon, and Josh Simpson point to a collective tradition that undergirds their contemporary explorations. Walter Goodridge and Tai Hazard invoke the art and architecture of another culture as they devise the shapes and proportions of their own work. Since they value the instruction of others, perhaps it's not surprising that all ten artists teach, or offer instructional workshops, or work with apprentices. "Passing on and enriching the culture of my craft," as Mark Shapiro puts it, is a legacy they take seriously.

My most unexpected discovery was the oft-heard message, reiterated in some way by each artist, that it is the body that learns and remembers the skills necessary to produce art. Mark Shapiro and Tai Hazard speak repeatedly of "honing hand skills" which then perform the movements flawlessly, allowing the mind the freedom to be inventive. Barry Moser speaks of "muscle memory" as the dependable source of his skills as an engraver, and Josh Simpson likens his glassblowing skills to dancing or successfully landing an airplane when "the body is allowed to remember what it can do, unimpeded by the rational mind." Rationality doesn't run the show. In fact, after what Tai Hazard calls the "practice, practice, practice stage," rationality is asked to step aside, providing the space for the freedoms and intuitive skills of the body to operate.

The body, I discovered, works with a kind of deliberateness when making art, calibrating the pace of the work to the difficulty of its execution. Watching Ken Salem meticulously match two pieces of spalted wood, or Sally Dillion arrange, then rearrange, study, then dismantle intricate pieces of a quilt, or Walter Goodridge turn a bowl on a lathe, patiently, delicately applying the abrading tool made me remember Thoreau's famous challenge: "Why should we be in such a desperate haste to succeed? Let a man step to the music which he hears, however measured or far away." Deliberateness in the artistic process is not some different drummer gesture, a nod in the direction of nonconformity. It flows, I see now, from honoring the body's pace, direction, and insight.

It would be easy to romanticize the artistic life, easy, that is, until one really listens to artists speak about the challenges they face. Most artists are up against the stark fact of financial insecurity all the time. Its jeopardy requires long hours and all the anxiety of "making a living mug by mug," as Mark Shapiro puts it. Age brings deteriorations to us all, but arthritis in the hands and dimming of the eyesight are special curses for those who depend upon the suppleness of their hands and the keenness of their sight. Almost invariably a conversation would end with an artist acknowledging that harder bridges to cross lay ahead. Yet they persist in what Carol Blinn calls "doing work we cannot live without." Their work condenses, crystallizes, and clarifies life in ways that seem to supersede the sacrifices.

I glimpsed one of those risky rewards when I asked each artist to provide a slide of a favorite piece of work and to attach a short description explaining its particular challenges. Although variety characterized their responses, I came to see that one of the unique gifts of making a one-of-a-kind piece was leaving something of yourself in the work itself. I'm not speaking here of those fuzzy notions of "self-expression" that sometimes clog writing textbooks. I mean actually transferring some part of the self to the work: the hand that shapes the clay, the eye that visualizes the wood grain, the wrist that cradles the composing stick. When you look at the work, it looks right back at you; it functions as both the mirror and the lamp.

I began the introduction of this book by suggesting that my original entree into the history of the Pioneer Valley came through its writers, particularly Dickinson, Hawthorne, Melville, and Thoreau, who chose to study the lineaments of the soul itself, to have it out on their own terms. Literature is my bedrock, my home ground. Moreoever, I have never made anything perfectly with my hands, despite a longing to do so. My life's work, teaching and writing, is its own kind of "making" I suppose, though its results land on multiple pages or walk in the shoes of former students.

Ever since I first read, as an enthralled teenager, Thoreau's description of cabin building at Walden Pond, I have imagined the gratifications of constructing even a ten-by-fifteen-foot structure. I thrilled to Thoreau's promise: "If you have built castles in the air, your work need not be lost; that is where they should be. Now put foundations under them." But I had trouble pouring the concrete.

Perhaps it is that very capacity to make something by hand, new and fresh, with something of yourself embedded in it that draws me to these artists with a mixture of respect and awe. Yet, as I have written this book, the line of demarcation I arbitrarily drew between literary seers and artist-makers has wavered. It grows fainter and fainter. For surely at the heart of each artistic endeavor is the centering clarity of work, a love of solitude, and a discipline that offers a way of being in the world while still being in touch with the soul.

When sculptor Anne Truitt was asked where she thought art came from, I heard Dickinson and Thoreau in her answer:

"I don't know. But I think it's possible to put oneself in the way of art in much the same way that cloistered devotees place themselves in the way of religious experience. Art comes, if we are blessed, . . . with a touch of grace. But we have to pay attention in order to notice the grace, or even perhaps to attract it."

ACKNOWLEDGMENTS

When I first explored the idea of doing a book about artists in the Pioneer Valley who handcraft beautiful pieces of art, a friend rolled her eyes and said: "Ten different artists meeting all those deadlines? That's a bit like trying to herd cats."

My primary thanks go to Tai, Walter, Carol, Barry, Sally, Josh, Ken, Susan, and both Marks—who, despite demanding work schedules, were generous with their time, kept all their deadlines, offered valuable slides and prints of original work, and enriched this book tenfold. The staff at Commonwealth Editions enthusiastically supported this project and, under the expert guidance of Webster Bull, produced a book worthy of its subjects. Mary Schjeldahl's photographic skill and warm friendship made our collaboration a delight. And the arts community in the Valley, particularly Michael Zibman of Silverscape Designs, Rich Michelson and Liz Finney of R. Michelson Galleries, and Geoffrey and Linda Post, codirectors of the Paradise City Arts Festival, offered valuable advice as I selected ten artists from a staggering pool of talent.

I'm fortunate to have an "extended family"—mentors, family, friends, colleagues—who read sections of almost everything I write, offering recommendations and their own special brands of encouragement. My thanks to Carol Booth, Dorothy Braham, Mary Jeanne Mullen Buck, Anne Eberle, Jane Garrett, Judith Hancock, Serena Hilsinger, Charles Ketcham, Tim Mullen, Beth Reynders, Victoria Safford, Chris Shipley, Bruce Wilcox, Kristin Woolever, and especially Lynn Walterick, whose editorial ear is pitch-perfect.

To Pam, Caleigh, and Brodie, co-explorers of the Pioneer Valley and all its riches, this book is for you.

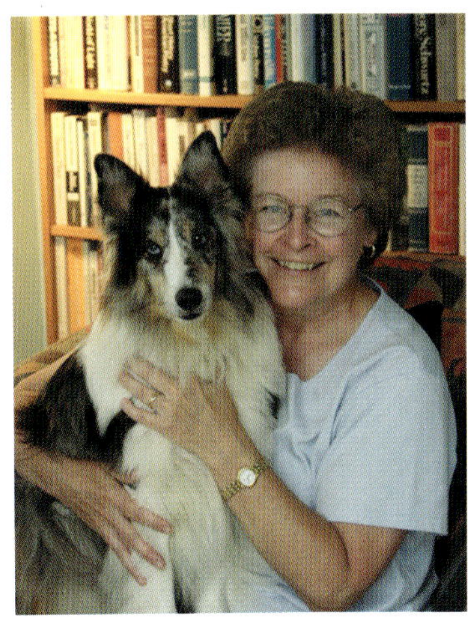

JEANNE BRAHAM received a Bachelor of Arts from the College of Wooster, a Master of Arts from the University of Pennsylvania, and a Doctor of Arts from Carnegie Mellon University. She has taught literature and creative writing at a number of colleges and universities, including Allegheny College, Smith College, Hampshire College, the University of New Hampshire, and Clark University. The author of two collections of poetry and three books of nonfiction, she is also the founding editor of Heatherstone Press, a fine arts poetry press. She lives in Sunderland, Massachusetts, on the banks of the Connecticut River.

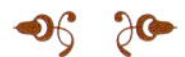

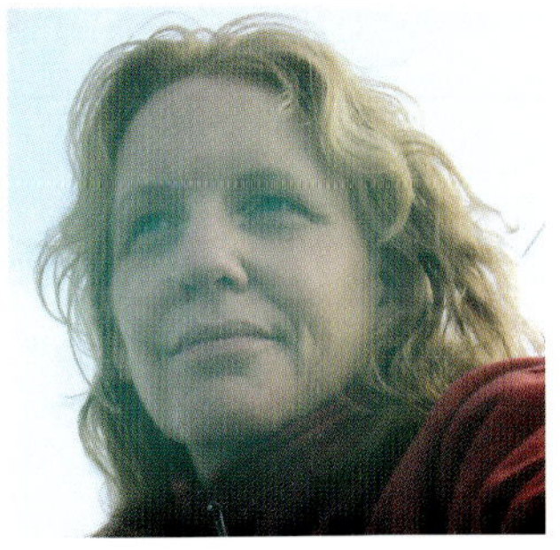

MARY SCHJELDAHL graduated with a fine arts degree in photography from Parsons School of Design in New York City. Exhibitions of her work have appeared in galleries in New York City and elsewhere. Her photographs have appeared in a wide range of journals, newspapers, and magazines, including *Orion Magazine, Boston Globe Magazine, Disney Magazine*, the *Los Angeles Times Sunday Magazine, Country Home*, and *Hope Magazine*. She lives in Worthington, Massachusetts, one of the hill towns encircling the Pioneer Valley.